Praise for *I*

"Read it, do it, and you will sell more."

—**Hermann W. Braun, Director of Category Management and Shopper Marketing, Ferrero Germany**

"This is a unique book that examines and explains the need for the measurement of actual shopper behavior in retail environments. Based on real shopper studies, this takes analysis beyond POS data. Herb Sorensen pays particular attention to precise measurement of non-intuitive aspects of shopper interaction with the shelf."

—**Franz A. Dill, Former Manager and Founder of Procter & Gamble's Retail Innovation Center**

"Herb Sorensen's ideas and observations about in-store shopper behavior have been instrumental in shaping my recent research. He has an uncanny ability to see beyond surface details and detect meaningful patterns of genuine interest to front-line managers and senior executives. It's great that so much of his wisdom—and that of other researchers he has influenced—is collected together here."

—**Peter Fader, Professor of Marketing, The Wharton School of the University of Pennsylvania**

"Every year retailers disrupt their customers by spending time, money, and resources remodeling stores. Before remodeling one more store, read what Herb Sorensen has learned about how customers shop and how you can use it to improve your customer's shopping performance and your earnings.

One hundred years ago retailers ran their stores by watching their customers closely. Somewhere during the last hundred years, spread sheets, slotting allowances, and quarterly performance replaced the basic principles of the business. Sorensen's book puts you back on the floor of the store and allows you to see how the customer sees your store. What Sorensen shows you will make your stores better and more efficient for the customer and will maximize the money you are investing in design and remodels."

—**Norm Myhr, Group Vice President Sales Promotion and Marketing, Fred Meyer**

"This book is priceless for anyone in retailing. It is based on 40 years of retail experience, and Herb Sorensen opens the doors to a new world. He serves us with masses of empirical data and examples, but also with new metrics and a new theory of shopper behavior. I am certain that he will challenge most retailers as well as researchers and force them to check if what he states can really be so. He challenged me, I had to check, and he was right!"

—Jens Nordfaült, Assistant Professor, Stockholm School of Economics; Dean, Nordic School of Retail Management; CEO, Hakon Swenson Research Foundation

"*Inside the Mind of the Shopper* is the preeminent handbook for any marketer or retailer seeking to understand why people do what they do when they shop. Armed with the knowledge in this book, marketers and retailers can work together to predict how shoppers will respond (or not!) to package and label design, selling messages, shelf plans, and the entire retail space."

—Matt Ohligschlager, Senior Manager, Consumer and Market Knowledge, Procter & Gamble

"A must read for anyone who is passionate about understanding shopping."

—Joe Radabaugh, Director, Shopper Marketing, Nestlé USA

"From his 40 years of observing shoppers, Herb Sorensen has given us the gift of understanding shoppers. Now, we clearly see that the store layouts merchants want are not what shoppers want. On the ground, managers THINK they know their shoppers, but anyone who follows Herb's handbook on shopper insights will know them a lot better."

—Joel Rubinson, Chief Research Officer, The Advertising Research Foundation

"Herb Sorensen is the dean of behaviorally responsive shopper marketing. Crammed with stats and crisp insights, his book guides retail professionals through the maze of motivations that lead shoppers to locate, stop, and buy."

—James Tenser, Principal, VSN Strategies

Inside the Mind of the Shopper

Inside the Mind of the Shopper

The Science of Retailing

Herb Sorensen, Ph.D

For information about buying this title in bulk quantities, or for special sales opportunites (which may include electronic versions; custom cover designs;and content particular to your business, training goals, marketing focus, or brand interests), please contact our corporate sales department at corpsales@pearsoned.com or (800) 382-3419. For government sales inquiries, please contact governmentsales@pearsoned.com. For questions about sales outside the U.S., please contact internationalpearsoned.com.

First Printing: May 2015

ISBN-10: 0-13-438590-X
ISBN-13: 978-0-13-438590-7

Pearson Education LTD.
Pearson Education Australia PTY, Limited.
Pearson Education Singapore, Pte. Ltd.
Pearson Education North Asia, Ltd.
Pearson Education Canada, Ltd.
Pearson Educación de Mexico, S.A. de C.V.
Pearson Education—Japan
Pearson Education Malaysia, Pte. Ltd.

Library of Congress Cataloging-in-Publication Data is on file.

Vice President, Publisher
Tim Moore

Associate Publisher and Director of Marketing
Amy Neidlinger

Editor
Steve Kobrin

Acquisitions Editor
Jennifer Simon

Editorial Assistant
Pamela Boland

Operations Manager
Gina Kanouse

Digital Marketing Manager
Julie Phifer

Publicity Manager
Laura Czaja

Assistant Marketing Manager
Megan Colvin

Cover Designer
Alan Clements

Managing Editor
Kristy Hart

Project Editor
Jovana San Nicolas-Shirley

Copy Editor
Water Crest Publishing

Proofreader
San Dee Phillips

Indexer
Erika Millen

Compositor
Nonie Ratcliff

Manufacturing Buyer
Dan Uhrig

Dedication

This book is dedicated to Bob Stevens of Procter & Gamble (P&G), the man who set me on the path of "active retailing" and who is also widely viewed as a pioneer in the field of shopper research.

He was a man of many talents: A consummate researcher, he was also an avid sports fan. Indeed, at 15, he began a short career as a professional wrestler, assuming the name "Rocky Stevens." Later in life, his love of basketball took him to Israel, Italy, and Alaska to cheer on his teams.

Bob was a devout Christian, a loving husband, father, and grandfather, and a philanthropist, too. He raised money for education and, post-retirement, taught and lectured often on market research and management, donating his honoraria to charity. For a time, he served on the board of Hope Cottage, a temporary shelter for abused, abandoned, or neglected children.

The greatest portion of his life, however, was spent at P&G where, beginning in 1951, he spent nearly 40 years as a consumer research manager. Bob was known as an inveterate people-watcher, fascinated by consumers' behavior both in-store and out, and especially their interaction with products.

His retirement did not put a stop to his professional involvement. He continued to write about marketing and research in a periodic newsletter called "Views from the Hills of Kentucky," which he emailed or faxed *gratis* to subscribers.

So, what made this man special? He was an advocate for the shopper, for understanding their needs and for doing the right thing as a researcher—often acting as a role model for his peers. He was always curious about what people *did* as opposed to what they *said*. And in many ways, his work has stood the test of time, as brands began to focus more on ethnography.

Bob would always dig a little deeper when it came to research. Bob Goodpaster, who is currently Vice President of Global Insights for The Hershey Company, recalls that when he worked with him at P&G, Bob would focus on research at one or two stores, giving people coupons to go in and buy products, while collecting their names and phone numbers for follow-up research.

What he was trying to do was to predict potential repeat purchasing, but working it out over a weekend—without having to wait months and months to read the normal statistical print-outs. He was *way* ahead of his time.

It couldn't have been easy because, as with any pioneer, there were those who were enthusiastic about change and those who were afraid of it. But Bob persevered, and rarely turned down the chance to innovate. For P&G, this resulted in insights that the company might never have achieved otherwise. Indeed, P&G is one of the most innovative research organizations around today—and Bob played a part in laying the foundations of continuing innovation.

He was an expert in understanding the relation between P&G products on the shelf and the shoppers walking by. He followed those shoppers home with their products to see how they actually used them. Harking back to the early days of his career, he pioneered the use of hall tests in the 1950s, seeing it as yet another way to get closer to consumers.

Bob's philosophy lies at the heart of this book, too. His enthusiasm for researching shoppers—for knowing what goes on when they enter a store—is translated in these pages into a modus operandi for retailers (and brand owners) who want to make the most of their businesses.

Earlier, I mentioned his newsletters, which inspired new ways of thinking and working. I include samples from two of his favorite topics in the Appendix, distinguishing between "testers" and "users" and the need for "assessment in context," and the full set is available online. Bob's views on these issues matched my own major concerns as a scientist transplanted to market research. We believe that customers should be studied in their native environment: This means researching supermarket shoppers in supermarkets; food service patrons in restaurants, schools, and other commercial and non-commercial locations; food service operators in their kitchens; schoolchildren in their schools; and so on. Also, we prefer direct observation of "users," and asking questions, converting them into "testers" as follow-ups, rather than as the foundation of the research.

Our learnings about the messy process of testing in context were inspired by Bob, and became integral to my business following discussions with him. It was Bob who turned my narrow focus from the shoppers and the products to the stores, their natural habitat. I hope that, from whatever lofty peak he's now operating, he feels that I'm still taking his work forward in the ongoing search for truth about shoppers.

Contents

Author's Notes and Acknowledgments

I was born at an early age....

What might have been seen as precocity in the first half of my life has evolved into a certain independence in this half. Here I want to give tribute to some of the key players in bringing this book to fruition.

From my mother, I inherited a drive for improvement, and from my father, hard work as the proper and justifying role of man. I met my wife when I was fourteen, and was blown away by her wise and serious essay on the stages of life, read by her to our English III class in high school. Approaching our fiftieth wedding anniversary, she has been the tether that kept me connected to those most important things in life. Five years after our first meeting, we had our first daughter Kris, while I was finishing my senior year in college.

All of my five children grew up inside the business that evolved to deliver this book. Kris, now a stay-at-home-mom, managed the operations side of the business during some of the most explosive growth we ever experienced. Beth, even as a pre-teen, was helping with keeping those rows and columns straight, in the days when we did manual tabulation of survey data. Later, she and I set a personal record of 130 respondents recruited and interviewed in one hectic day in Santa Monica.

Jon is the philosopher-musician-writer who helped me begin contributing reports and articles to the marketing research press. This work laid the foundations of this book, helping me to think through some of the issues covered here. James is the right hand that built Sorensen Associates, "The in-store research company®," which the world has come to know. He is the one who transmuted my scientific curiosity into something of practical value for our clientele, which has swelled under his ministrations.

Paul is an award-winning nuclear physicist who wrote the software for our TURF analysis (Total Unduplicated Reach and Frequency). We continue to use the procedures he developed for shopper flow analysis in our PathTracker® Tool Suite.

Beyond the core of my family, the towering influence from my early professional years was Lloyd Ingraham, my major professor at the University of California at Davis. His was an open and searching mind that encouraged the same for me. What an incredible experience, to be given free range and funding to follow my nose into nuclear quadrupole resonance, chick embryo metabolism, the quantum chemistry of small ring heterocycles, the role of thiamine in muscular dystrophy, and radio-carbon and dendrochronology—all resulting in peer-reviewed scientific papers in one three-year period.

Leaping forward nearly 30 years found me with an eclectic history encompassing university faculty positions, board-certified clinical chemistry, which evolved through a food laboratory and sensory science to market research. The logical connection through all this is curiosity.

In 2000, three things converged—my long-standing curiosity about the overall movement of shoppers through stores, my acquaintance with Peter Fader at Wharton, and client support by Sandy Swan at Dr. Pepper/7UP for an initiative to conduct the study. Although a few others followed, it was Sandy's immediate financial encouragement that launched PathTracker®, the most extensive study of shopper paths (and much more) ever conducted. Sandy was with me on the early work when the insights were accumulating, but the knowledge of how to use the insights profitably was slow to coalesce.

And then, Peter Fader's immediate and enthusiastic support for the project rendered the objective, academic *imprimatur* that I valued more than the money. His practical views on the relation of online and offline retailing are covered in our interview in Chapter 7, "Integrating Online and Offline Retailing: An Interview with Professors Peter Fader (The Wharton School) and Wendy Moe (University of Maryland)."

Mike Twitty of Unilever was another major influence. Mike and I both participated in the first IIR Shopper Insights Conference (2001), and I recognized early on that Mike was a *serious* student of the shopper. Mike Twitty has had the "quick trip" as a focus for several years, and my own overwhelming data forced me to recognize the unclaimed potential in this area. Mike is making a tremendous contribution to the entire industry through the insights he shares from this work in Chapter 6, "The Quick-Trip Paradox: An Interview with Unilever's Mike Twitty."

I've mentioned the role of curiosity in my career and this book. Science is, of course, another prominent motif. But *independence* is perhaps as important. Not caring what anyone else thinks is a strength and flaw encouraged by a decade or more of living, like Thoreau, in my own mountain-forest semi-isolation. My independence, however, is tempered by a healthy dose of personal insecurity, which always secretly seeks confirmation and approval. But I am very picky about whose approval and confirmation I care about.

This is the significance of Fader, Twitty; and later of Bill Bean, then at Pepsi but now at Colgate; then Mark Heckman, now (and again) at Marsh; and even later of Cliff McGregor of Nestlé; and, finally, Siemon Scammell-Katz of ID Magasin, now a colleague at TNS/Kantar. In any budding and exciting field like "shopper," there are always plenty of thin poseurs. But these folks are genuine gold, having their own independent and advanced expertise in the shopper that I know and care about.

Bill Bean, while at Pepsi, sponsored a study of four supermarkets using the RFID tracking technology, while it was still cutting/bleeding edge. Bill took the raw data from those four stores and did his own independent study, using intelligent agent modeling with Icosystem, which confirmed and went beyond many of the things I was learning myself. (The Wharton group under Fader has also operated independently, following its own curiosity and analytical strengths.)

Mark Heckman worked with me closely as an associate for a couple years before returning to Marsh Supermarkets. He brought a real-world retailer perspective to our research. This allowed PathTracker® to become not just a tool looking from the outside in on the business, but from the inside looking out. In Chapter 9, "Insights into Action: A Retailer Responds: An Interview with Mark Heckman of Marsh Supermarkets," he discusses how a retailer has specifically benefited from implementing the principles in this book.

Siemon Scammell-Katz is the first person I ever met who knew many of the principles and truths that were emerging from PathTracker® but had no prior exposure to the intricacies of our work. His knowledge was a result of having spent more than a decade studying shoppers' behavior on a tenth of a second by tenth of a second basis (fixation by fixation) from point-of-focus eye tracking studies, primarily in Europe. Siemon's independent work not only served as confirmation, but also stimulated me to a renewed interest in eye tracking, particularly linking the footpath to the eye path.

Finally, Cliff McGregor at Nestlé and I have had many illuminating (to me) discussions. These interested me greatly, initially, because of Cliff's former participation in the Envirosell organization in Australia before he joined Nestlé. I've mentioned in the book my great respect for Paco

Underhill's work, although we have never been connected professionally, other than my reading his books and sitting in his audiences.

Cliff has done me the kindness of reading the entire first draft and commenting, to my profit, on various features. I spent a very pleasant day in 2007 chatting with Cliff about our mutual views on shoppers. This was very helpful because of my own newness to the global scene and his wide experience of global retailing, as well as a more detailed view into the cultural anthropological approach to studying shoppers. The anthropological view has been further enhanced by Emil Morales' contribution on multicultural retailing, which he discusses in Chapter 8, "Multicultural Retailing: An Interview with Emil Morales, Senior Vice President of TNS Multicultural."

In this sense, Siemon, Cliff, and Emil have all enhanced my own study and focus by broadening my scope to a bigger picture, as well as a more detailed focus on the individual shopper.

In my mind, I have something of an artificial boundary between myself and "my" company, which in reality has been run for quite a few years by my son, James. But at the same time, there is an obvious connection, beyond family. Frankly, I could never have learned what I have about shoppers if I had stayed tethered to our clients' questions and interests. On the other hand, had the company not focused on those, we wouldn't exist. It is James and his staff that have mediated the learnings from Path-Tracker® to the world of our clients. But James has been the stern "client" that always disciplines me with, "So what?" And it has not been an indifferent "So what." This is why Chapter 5, "Brands, Retailers, and Shoppers: Why the Long Tail Is Wagging the Dog," is in reality a collaboration between myself, James, Siemon, and Ginger Sack, our senior researcher on the client side. So, as I have learned from all the others, James and Ginger have taught me most how to introduce science to our marketer clients.

Of course, many at TNS Sorensen have played crucial roles in supporting my studies, and I thank them all—but two have been the heavy-lifters in research and development. Dave Albers is the concept and numbers genius that always improves every idea I bring him, and Marcus Geroux is the creative talent who does the same with devices, electronics, and anything requiring "making." I told Marcus once that he must have apprenticed with James Bond's "Q." Both have played key roles in one or more of the suite of patents underlying the PathTracker® Tool Suite.

My sincere thanks to the giants mentioned here, upon whose shoulders I have stood.

Finally, I must thank my colleagues at TNS, particularly Sean Hosey, who introduced me to Laura Mazur and Louella Miles, who spent the better part of a year coaxing and encouraging me in the writing of the book, drafting content from my interviews, rewriting and stitching together a vast quilt from the multifarious pieces I had assembled willy-nilly over the years. It really was a surprise to me to learn how different writing a book is than assembling a series of articles. However, the result of all this was a very fine *scientific* document, organized in my own inimitable style.

It was then that the publisher, Pearson and Prentice Hall, stepped in, along with Robert Gunther, to reorganize the content and create a book of wider interest to a broader readership. All the while, the steady support of Jerry (Yoram) Wind and Steve Kobrin, Editors at Prentice Hall, encouraged perseverance. Jennifer Simon and her supporting team at Pearson have played the final role in creating what I think of as a very fine book. Of course, I retain all responsibility for the content of the final document, so send any brickbats my way. Kudos to the rest!

About the Author

Herb Sorensen is a preeminent authority on observing and measuring shopping behavior and attitudes within the four walls of the store. He has worked with Fortune 100 retailers and consumer packaged-goods manufacturers for more than 35 years, studying shopper behavior, motivations, and perceptions at the point of purchase. Sorensen's patented shopper-tracking technology PathTracker® is helping to revolutionize retail marketing strategies from a traditional "product-centric" perspective to a new "shopper-centric" focus. As *Baseline* magazine commented, "Herb Sorensen and Paco Underhill are the yin and yang of observational research."

Herb has conducted studies in North America, Europe, Asia, Australia, and South America. His research has been published in *AMA's Marketing Research*, *The Journal of Advertising Research*, *FMI Advantage Magazine*, *Progressive Grocer*, and *Chain Drug Review*, and he has been utilized as an expert source for *The Wall Street Journal*, *Supermarket News*, and *BusinessWeek*. Additionally, he is currently a panelist of Retail Wire's "Brain Trust."

Herb was named one of the top 50 innovators of 2004 by *Fast Company Magazine*, and shared the American Marketing Association's 2007 EXPLOR Award for technological applications that advance research, with Peter Fader and his group at the Wharton School of Business of the University of Pennsylvania. Herb has a Ph.D. in Biochemistry.

Preface

Rethinking Retail

"When you cannot express it in numbers, your knowledge is of a meager and unsatisfactory kind."

—Lord Kelvin

The supermarket is my laboratory. After earning my Ph.D. in biochemistry and working for a brief period in the food industry, I traded a lab bench for the aisles of the supermarket. At that time, the supermarket was a black box. Manufacturers and retailers were concerned about how to get shoppers into the door and make them aware of products before their trips, but they assumed that they understood what happened when the shopper was inside. Our research, discussed in this book, shows that in many cases they were wrong.

In the early 1970s, I left my practice as a board-certified clinical chemist and started a small laboratory providing a range of services, primarily to the agricultural and consumer packaged goods industries. One of the services that we provided was sensory evaluation—consumer taste test surveys. Following the example of universities, our "tasters" were college and university students. I initially started doing in-store research because a client said that he didn't think the opinions of college students, with their well-known penchant for pizza and ramen noodles, were very representative of typical supermarket shoppers.

Being a scientist, rather than a market researcher, it never occurred to me *not* to interview supermarket shoppers. I approached the manager of a local supermarket, and he readily gave me permission to interview his shoppers. Remember, this was more than 30 years ago, and the local

Albertsons manager had an amazing degree of autonomy. When we were in the store, we found that there were many other interesting questions to study.

I pursued the in-store research niche—first as a solo consultant and then as the founder and president of Sorensen Associates, "The In-store Research Company®," and more recently, as Global Scientific Director, Retail and Shopper Insights at TNS, a global research and information services firm. We are now a part of the even larger conglomerate WPP, with a focus on advertising and communications. Although most of our experience is with supermarkets and brand manufacturers of fast-moving consumer packaged goods, we have found our core insights hold for work with supercenters, drugstores, convenience stores, auto parts retailers, building centers, consumer electronics, phone stores, and many other retailers or products. We have completed studies in a variety of channels on every continent except Africa and Antarctica, and the paradigm, metrics, and insights are as relevant elsewhere as in the U.S. (with some differences, as we will examine later). Over the years, we came to appreciate the value of conducting research in the store environment, rather than just doing research about the store, products, and shoppers.

We decided to study what shoppers actually did in the store, what they looked at, how they moved through the store, and what they bought. We examined strategies that could be used to increase sales, testing these approaches in the laboratory of real stores with actual shoppers. We traveled with customers down thousands of miles of supermarket aisles and analyzed millions of hours of shopping to help retailers create more effective stores and approaches. We found that simple interventions could have dramatic effects, but only if you understood how shoppers think. And some widely used strategies have little impact on the behavior of most shoppers, so we also helped retailers stop throwing money away.

As a pioneer in the field of in-store research, I have had the opportunity to see retailing go through many changes—including the emergence of new technologies and online retailing. As the industry continues to change, however, the basic insights from our research continue to hold true. And in a more complex and dynamic environment, understanding shopper behavior may be even more important.

I have spent millions of dollars of my own money doing some of this research, and the world's top brands and forward-thinking retailers have spent millions more on specific projects and PathTracker® studies. We have looked at every square-inch of these stores and analyzed millions of shopping trips on a second-by-second basis, using the best technology at our disposal. The results, to the extent that the information is not proprietary, are contained within the covers of this book.

I am grateful to the many managers who embraced and supported this work, even when it was unproven. I am particularly fortunate to have worked with Bob Stevens, to whom this book is dedicated. He had recently retired after 40 years in market research for Procter & Gamble, and taught me to go far beyond the product-shopper dimension mentioned previously. This, in turn, led to the development of my current holistic view of the shopper experience, including the invention of the PathTracker® suite of tools, metrics, and a scientific paradigm for the subject of shopping. Finally, I am grateful for the fine work by other pioneers, such as Paco Underhill and Siemon Scammel-Katz.

Along the way, we have faced resistance to this approach. As researchers at one of the largest supermarket chains in the world told us: "We do not interview our shoppers in-store, but conduct phone or Internet surveys of them." Interviewing shoppers outside of the store is like trying to understand the movements of a flock of birds by observing a specimen in a natural history museum. It is shocking to me, but not at all exceptional.

This book offers managers in retail firms, or companies that sell products through retail, valuable insights into what happens to their customers when they walk through the front door of the store. Companies that spend countless dollars getting the customer to this point often look away just at this critical moment, giving scant attention to the "last mile" of retailing. Retailers and brand owners know all about who the people are going into the store, and what they are carrying home from the store, and a lot about what they are doing at home. But I stake my career to a large degree on the fact that they know very little about the *process* that occurs in the store. (As I will consider later, this lack of knowledge might be due in part to the structure of the industry, which means retailers and manufacturers get more out of interacting with one another than with customers in the aisles.) This book also offers anyone who has shopped or wants to understand the shopping experience, research-based insights into the habits of the shopper.

On the following pages, we explore some of the key insights from this work—the quick trip, three moments of truth for the shopper, in-store "migration" patterns, and how to put products in the path of customers through anticipatory retailing. We also look at how manufacturers and retailers can collaborate better in shaping flow and adjacency to sell more products in stores. In the second part of the book, we offer insights from a series of interviews with executives and experts on specific topics related to in-store retailing: deeper insights on the quick trip, the integration of online and offline retailing, multicultural retailing, and a retailer's perspective on the issues presented in this book. Whether you are running or designing stores, building brands, or merely want a deeper understanding of shopping behavior, this book will challenge the way you look at shopping.

In a certain sense, the shoppers' eyes offer a window into our entire society. As I realized in four decades of this work, retailing is at the cutting edge of social evolution because it brings people and the things they *must have* together. This is where the dreams and aspirations of consumers and the messages of brand owners intersect in a concrete action to make a purchase. If you want to understand our society, taking a trip with a shopper down a supermarket aisle is a very good start. I invite you to join me on this journey through the modern supermarket. I think you will be surprised at what we find.

—Herb Sorensen, Ph.D.

Introduction

Twenty Million Opportunities to Buy

The great obstacle to discovering the shape of the Earth, the continents, and the oceans was not ignorance but the illusion of knowledge. Imagination drew in bold strokes, instantly serving hopes and fears, while knowledge advanced by slow increments and contradictory witnesses.

—Daniel Boorstin, *The Discoverers*, 1993

A woman in her 30s moves through the aisles of a Stop & Shop outside of Boston. She was selected for our study because she planned to purchase dish detergent, one of the types of products of interest to our client. We fitted her with specially designed glasses connected to a device that records her field of vision every 3/25ths of a second and relays it to a computer (see Figure I.1). The glasses also reflect the corneal image of her eyes so we can track exactly what she is looking at in her field of vision as she moves through the supermarket aisles. Instead of *watching* shoppers, we actually *see what they see* and focus on.

After the images are overlaid with crosshairs indicating where her gaze is focused, they are analyzed by technicians in India (see Figure I.2). We know where she went, what she looked at, and what she did as a result. We are not asking her what she did after the fact. We are not just observing her. We are seeing through her eyes. Short of crawling inside her head (and we are actually beginning to do this), this is as close as anyone has ever gotten to understanding the complexity of the shopping experience and what shoppers actually do in their natural habitat. Given that 90 percent of all sensory input comes through vision, understanding what shoppers see offers a pretty good view of their thinking.

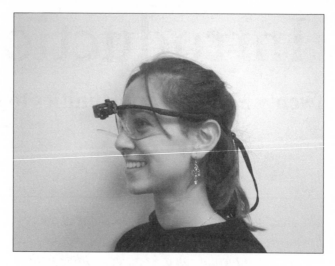

Figure I.1 Specially designed glasses record the eye movements of the shopper as she walks through the store.

Point of focus

Figure I.2 The images from the glasses show the field of vision, and crosshairs indicate the shopper's point of focus at each step, second by second, along the route through the store.

In this one-minute journey (images from the first 30 seconds are shown in Figure I.3), our subject moves quickly past shelves of paper towels, tissues, and napkins, scanning left and right without stopping. She is on a mission. At mid-aisle, she looks at the end cap display on the left. Then, she looks all the way to the end of the aisle, perhaps to get her bearings, scanning the very bottom shelf of the left side of the aisle. She swings her gaze across the aisle to the bottom shelf of the right side, and then moves up along the second shelf. Her gaze zigzags to the top and then to the bottom. She hits a display of brushes and other cleaning products and that breaks her path, so she goes to the left side again. She reaches rows of detergents and stops her cart, scanning rapidly up and down the shelves. Just before she grabs the detergent, she looks down at her cart where a store circular sits on the seat. Could she be checking on the brand in the circular before grabbing the product? She leans a bottle of green detergent forward just before taking it off the shelf. Then, she puts back the green bottle, looks up to the top shelf, and pulls down a pink bottle to put into her cart.

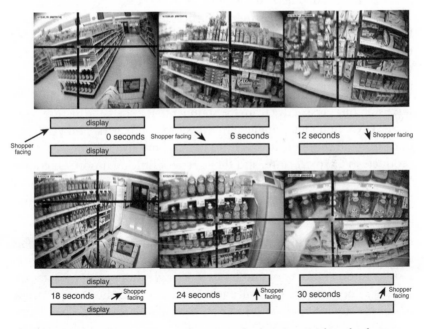

Figure I.3 Images from a 30-second segment of a shopping trip show the shopper checking the end cap, entering the aisle, scanning right and left, and making a purchase. The diagrams below each figure indicate the way the shopper is facing between the two aisles.

This video clip of her passage down one aisle of paper goods and detergents lasts just half a minute. In thirty seconds, her gaze has passed over hundreds of products; she has considered a few and selected one. She has evolved from a visitor to a shopper to a buyer.

I often tell clients that there is a whole book in this one-minute clip. In a real sense, the volume you are holding now is that book.

Twenty Million Seconds: Shopper Time Is Mostly Wasted

Twenty million seconds. That is the time all customers collectively spend in a typical supermarket every week based on our measures across many stores. Each of those seconds is an opportunity to sell. That is 20 million opportunities a week to sell something. But the tragedy of modern retail is that most of those moments are wasted because retailers and manufacturers by and large do not know what the shopper is doing during these moments. Retailers focus on traffic but traffic in itself never buys anything; it is traffic investing time that becomes shopping. We have found that about 80 percent of shoppers' time is spent simply in moving from place to place in the store, not looking at and purchasing items, which means that most of the shopper's precious time and attention in the store is spent *not shopping*.

If we shift our perspective from the shopper to the shelf, the picture is just as bleak. We find that a single item in a store might attract only 300 seconds from all shoppers in an entire week, about five minutes. All those products in a typical store, and they get very little attention. Of course, as we will discuss later, some products get much more attention—not necessarily because of the product itself but often due to its location in the store.

In comparison to that huge number—20 million seconds—the number of purchases on most shopping trips is remarkably small. In fact, the most common number of purchases by a single shopper on most trips is just one. All those seconds, all those products, and the shopper walks out of the supermarket with just one item. Think about it. The average supermarket might stock 30,000 to 50,000 SKUs, and yet this shopper walks past them all to emerge with a single item. In a year, the average household buys just 300 different items. Shoppers are forced to wade into this thick jungle of offerings to find the handful of precious items that they truly want. We all know the jungle can be a lonely and dangerous place. Many shoppers are lost there.

This is the tragedy of modern retail. The shopper comes to the store to buy things. The retailer creates stores to sell things. Manufacturers create products to sell. Yet most of the shopper's time in the store is spent *not* buying. Shoppers and products long for each other, like Romeo and Juliet, but are held apart by forces greater than themselves. As we will discuss, some of these forces that keep shoppers from shopping are a result of the relationship between retailers and manufacturers, which means that more of the retailer's profits come from brand promotions than from shoppers themselves. This has led to a great emphasis on promotional dollars at the sacrifice of an attention to shoppers. This, in the long run, hurts both retailers and manufacturers, as well as, obviously, shoppers themselves. This relationship is why both retailers and manufacturers have paid far too little attention to shopping behavior. But it also means that there are tremendous opportunities to improve sales and profits by understanding shoppers better.

Table I.1 Lost Opportunities

The Facts	
1 quadrillion	The number of seconds all shoppers spend in all stores, globally, every year (not including automotive)
20 million	The number of those seconds shoppers spend in a single typical supermarket or supercenter in a single week
70 percent	The share of the shoppers' field of vision that is filled with commercial messages, including packages, on average
3 hundred	The number of seconds all shoppers spend in a give store, on average, on any single item, in a single week

(continued)

Table I.1 Lost Opportunities *(continued)*

The Facts	
80 percent	The share of the shoppers' time that is spent navigating the store instead of actually considering items for purchase
3 hundred	The number of different items a typical household buys in an entire year, only about half of those month after month

Brand owners have invested a great deal in understanding consumers outside the store, but how people behave in stores is quite different from what these studies outside show. There is no substitute for watching shoppers in the aisles of actual stores. People do not become real shoppers until they enter the store and cease to be shoppers when they leave the store. Forget what you know about consumers before they walk in the door of a store. Just as examining a military leader's strategy will tell you very little about what actually happens on the battlefield, no amount of shopper knowledge derived from outside-the-store measures will tell you about what will happen in the store. *Shopper insights are specifically about behaviors within the store's four walls.*[1]

> *The tragedy of modern retail is that most of the shopper's time in the store is spent not buying or selling. Of all the products on the shelves, only a small number account for most sales.*

Time Is Money: Shopper Seconds per Dollar

The millions of lost buying opportunities are very important. If we look at the whole shopping trip, the critical issue is not merely sales per visit but *seconds per dollar*. How long does it take shoppers in the store to spend a dollar? Across many studies, I have found a basic principle: The faster you close sales—the less time wasted for the shopper—the more sales you will make. In fact, when we charted this effect across a series of typical stores, we found that the efficiency of the shopping trip was directly related to overall store sales, as shown in Figure I.4. Given this data, does it make sense to force the shopper to walk through the entire store to find a quart of milk, thinking you might sell something else along the way? Or should you get them buying as quickly as possible and build momentum?

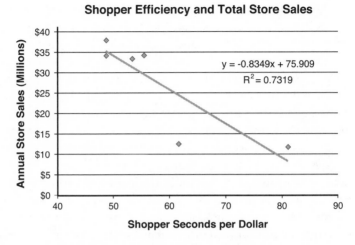

Shopper Efficiency and Total Store Sales

$$y = -0.8349x + 75.909$$
$$R^2 = 0.7319$$

Figure I.4 The faster shoppers spend, the higher total store sales.

As this figure illustrates, time really is money. The more quickly shoppers can make purchases, the greater the total store sales. In this sample, by shaving off 30 seconds per dollar, stores have doubled sales. This means that what goes on inside the store—including how the store is designed and what selection is offered and where—has a tremendous impact on sales. Following shoppers around on the trips through stores can reveal a great deal about how to make stores more profitable.

Leaving Money in the Aisles: The $80 Million Question

Retailers and manufacturers who understand what goes on inside the store can use this knowledge to increase their sales by fivefold. Because the typical supermarket does $10 million to $30 million in annual sales, wouldn't one doing $100 million in sales suggest something beyond extraordinary? In fact, a great deal of my thinking about supermarket design is influenced by the roughly $80 million of extra sales the typical supermarket leaves on the table. A great example of the potential can be seen in Stew Leonard's stores, with their $100 million in annual sales. Although Stew Leonard touts his world-class customer service as the secret of his success, there are two factors that amount to Stew Leonard dealing himself four aces hand after hand, and then thinking his winning is strictly due to his skill at playing the game. These four aces are founded on bedrock principles of shopping behavior. Stew Leonard's first two aces are the use of a serpentine path, which involves a single wide aisle that snakes its way past the merchandise through most of the store. The serpentine path eliminates the question: Where do I need to go next? You are going exactly where everyone else is going—right down this very wide aisle. This reduces navigational angst for shoppers. The second two aces are the reduction of shopper choice by pruning down his products to less than 2,000 individual items (SKUs) in the store, compared to 30,000 to 50,000 items in "competitive" stores. Stuffing the store with massive choices is unwelcome and unhelpful to shoppers, whereas it may be attractive to brand partners, particularly when what shoppers really want and need is buried in this indiscriminate mass. Although variety may help attract customers to the store, it often creates a barrier to shoppers. Through his store design, Stew Leonard makes sure that the right products show up in your field of vision by the time you get to the checkout. This reduces a second kind of shopper angst: choice angst.

Removing all this angst (choice angst and navigational angst) means that the shopper moves along at a steady pace—I'm told the shopping trip is actually *faster* than in a full supermarket—thinking about nothing except whether to put this or that into the basket. The result of this brilliant plan is an *extra* $80 million of sales each year, all put in the basket one item at a time by shoppers engrossed with nothing but putting items in the basket. No need to look over *huge* quantities of merchandise of no interest to you or your fellow shoppers. No need to "hunt" for anything. This means fewer shopper seconds per dollar and a resulting leap in annual store sales.

This serpentine path is not the only solution, as we will discuss later, but it does illustrate the potential of working with, rather than against, shopper behavior. This recognition of superior shopper strategy, of course, is not to underrate the truly world-class service that Stew Leonard regularly provides to shoppers, to which he credits his success. I believe this is a chicken-and-egg situation. If you are cranking $100 million in sales (admittedly running hard to do it), it's no wonder that you can go more than the extra mile with *all* your shoppers. Trust me, if you delivered Stew Leonard's service in your typical supermarket, you *would* get a significant bump in sales, *but it wouldn't be an extra $80 million!* To get that kind of performance, you have to rethink the total shopping experience.

I'm not surprised that retailers haven't leapt on the Stew Leonard's model. After all, they didn't leap on the Wal-Mart model or the convenience store model. Tesco's Fresh & Easy in the U.S., and the European discounters Lidl and Aldi, are pursuing the limited selection strategy. Echoes of Stew Leonard's model can be seen in HEB's Central Market designs, built on a serpentine model with a side warehouse area to accommodate the missing SKUs of a big store. Stew Leonard's now also has a "warehouse" area on the side, at the end of the trip, where shoppers can browse for those less-needed items. It makes the store more attractive without hectoring the shopper with massive amounts of merchandise in which they have no interest.

Planning Our Trip

On the following pages, we will take a journey through the store—and the mind of the shopper. As shown in Figure I.5, which highlights some key insights from Part I, "Active Retailing," we will consider diverse aspects of this journey, including the rise of the quick trip, moments of truth in the aisle that lead to purchases, migration patterns through the store, principles of active retailing, and the challenge of managing the big head (the few products shoppers buy frequently) and the long tail (the many products retailers stock). Before rolling down the aisle, let us briefly survey the path ahead.

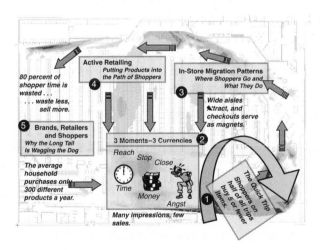

Figure I.5 Planning our trip through the book

Shoppers Make Small Trips to Large Stores

In observing the behavior of thousands of shoppers, letting shoppers group themselves according to behavior, we have identified three primary types of shoppers, as follows:[2]

- **Quick:** As noted previously, the number of products purchased most commonly on a shopping trip is one. These shoppers spend a short time in a small area, with a relatively slow walking speed but high spending speed. A third of all trips to the supermarket result in only one or two items being purchased, with fully half of all trips consisting of five or fewer items purchased.

- **Fill-in:** These shoppers visit about a fifth of the store, have a slightly faster—but still slow—walking speed and an average spending speed.

- **Stock-up:** These shoppers cover a larger area, walk more quickly, but have a lower spending speed.

Although most retail stores are designed for large stock-up shopping trips, most shopping trips are "quick trips," when shoppers buy only one or two items. In fact, shopping trips for 1 to 5 items typically generate a third of dollar sales. This is a mismatch between shoppers and stores that convenience stores have exploited, but other retailers have been slow to recognize. As retailers make bigger and bigger stores, they make it harder for quick trippers. As discussed previously, the average household purchases only 300 different products a year. Shoppers are purchasing these "big head" products—the small group of products that account for most of sales—while stores are stocked to the brim with "long tail" products. Retailers need to limit or manage these long tail products effectively, so they do not confuse or overwhelm the shopper.

One of the most important findings from this work is that quick trippers are *not* price sensitive. This has enormous implications for promotional strategies—many of which are a waste of money. Retailers are throwing away their discounts and coupons: Quick-trip shoppers who account for a large share of purchases are *price insensitive,* so price cuts do not change their behavior. In Chapter 1, "The Quick Trip: Eighty Percent of Shopper Time Is Wasted," we consider these three types of shoppers in more detail, particularly the quick-trip shopper. If half of all trips are quick trips, yet most stores are designed for stock-up purchasers, it is no wonder that stores underperform.

Three Moments of Truth and Three Currencies

Retailers and manufacturers typically focus on purchases and products, but the shopping experience is much richer and more complex. If shoppers, as we have found, spend only 20 percent of their time in-store actually selecting merchandise for purchase, what are they doing with the other 80 percent of their time? In our opening example, we saw how the woman in the Stop & Shop moved through three critical stages of shopping: reach, stop, and close. Her attention was caught by the product (reach), she stopped her shopping cart to look at it but also scanned other products around it on the shelf (stop), and she chose a particular bottle of detergent (closing the sale). These correspond to three in-store "moments of truth:" exposures, impressions, and sales. This is the process by which all in-store sales are made. Although retailers pay the most attention to the purchase itself, they need to understand this entire process.

Shoppers are spending more than money in the store. They are also spending their time and racking up angst. These are the three currencies of shopping. In addition to looking at what shoppers take out of their wallets, we also need to consider what they invest in time and angst in the experience. As we discussed, this angst can come from navigation (making products hard to find in the store) and from choice (overwhelming shoppers with too many choices). To understand shoppers, retailers and brand owners need to understand the entire shopping experience and the three currencies shoppers are spending in the store, as we consider in Chapter 2, "Three Moments of Truth and Three Currencies."

> *Shoppers are spending more than money in the store. They are also spending their time and racking up angst.*

Migration Patterns: Where Shoppers Go and What They Do

In addition to studying shopper segments, we also study the broader "migration patterns" of shoppers throughout the store, as illustrated in Figure I.6. Anchored by the entrance and exit, we observe predictable flows of traffic throughout the store. These flows are very hard to alter—although this can be done, particularly with store design. But you can also understand these flows and use a retail strategy that is designed to meet the shoppers where they naturally travel. This is what retailers do in deciding where to build their stores—looking for high-traffic areas or intersections of major interstates—but they rarely pay the same attention to actual traffic flows within the store, as we will consider in Chapter 3, "In-Store Migration Patterns: Where Shoppers Go and What They Do."

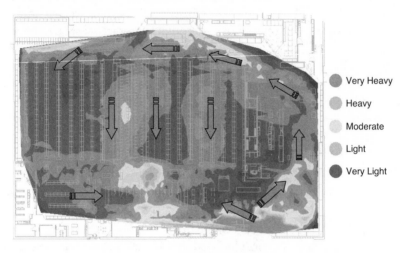

Figure I.6 Shoppers follow predictable paths through the store and some areas (darker shading) receive much heavier traffic than others.

The location of the entrance and the exit, as well as the location of wider aisles, largely defines this flow. Shoppers are used to coming in through a right entrance and making a counterclockwise sweep through the store—and they are somewhat resistant to changing these features as well. On the other hand, once managers understand these patterns, they can use this knowledge to put products in the path of shoppers.

The Holy Grail of Retailing: Taking Products to the Shoppers

We have found that it is hard to get shoppers to go to a specific point in the store, even if you throw money at them to do so. Time-pressured shoppers are less and less willing to invest *time* in the store to go that extra mile to connect with the products. As a result, those retailers who succeed in the future will be those who take control of that final mile in the store, by getting the right merchandise to the right shoppers at the right time. Retailers have to understand *where* the shoppers are spending their time in the store to make relevant offers where they actually are, rather than frustrate them by making them hunt for products.

Taking products to shoppers in the store represents a fundamental shift from the way most retailers and manufacturers think about retailing. In the early days of retail, shopkeepers actively waited on customers, assisting them with their selections and purchases. Then came self-service retailing. With the advent of the modern supermarket, interaction was no longer necessary, and turning the process over to the shopper reaped tremendous productivity gains. The supermarket became a mini-warehouse for the community. If the shoppers were taking care of themselves, retailers assumed they could take a passive role. Put the right products on the shelves, organize them by category, and turn the shoppers loose to find their way. This passive approach opened the way for smaller convenience stores, pioneered by gasoline service stations, which offered a limited selection of grocery items to customers.

Today, there is no shopkeeper to help customers make a purchase, but there is a different kind of active role for the retailer. It is actively understanding where shoppers are headed and actively making sure that they run into the product(s) they need and you want to sell. This is "postmodern active retailing." Getting products to people when and where they want them in the store is a strategy that requires detailed knowledge and insight of shoppers based on tracking what and where they buy on a trip-by-trip basis. For example, shoppers who buy candy on impulse in convenience stores usually come for a beverage. A candy maker seeking to increase its sales placed its product on the path to beverages and reduced the variety of offerings to simplify the choices. As a result, sales in the category increased by 3.3 percent and brand sales rose by 6.6 percent.

Through my own studies and other research on shopping behavior, I formulated "The Holy Grail of Retailing," as follows:

- To know exactly what each shopper wants, or may buy, as they come through the front door.

- To deliver that to them right away, accepting their cash quickly and speeding them on their way.

This goal reflects a different kind of active role for the retailer. Instead of a physical clerk taking products from shelves and presenting them to customers, the modern retailer takes an active role by superior understanding of shopper behavior and by creating the right store design, navigation, and selection so shoppers are presented with what they want when they want it. To the extent that retailers can achieve this goal, they will be rewarded in higher sales and profits. We will consider these strategies of "active retailing" in Chapter 4, "Active Retailing: Putting Products into the Path of Shoppers."

Online retailers face similar challenges, such as the problem of the abandoned Internet shopping cart, with a successful sale often requiring the vendor to identify early in the online browsing experience exactly what shoppers are looking for, and then serve it up to them quickly. But just as the online merchant monitors the click-click-click of the online browser/shopper, so too can the bricks-and-mortar merchant monitor the click-click-click of shoppers in the store, assess what they need or might want, and make appropriate offers. Active retailing is as much a state of mind as a set of specific methods or measures. Online is leading the way, conceptually, for what offline bricks-and-mortar retailers must do to gain or keep the leading edge.

Without at least a rudimentary knowledge of these issues—which this book provides—retailers and brand owners have no option but to continue to operate passively within the store. No amount of shopper knowledge derived from outside-the-store measures will do. The modern battle for retail ascendancy will be won *inside* the store. Outside-the-store factors will continue to influence what goes on inside, but they'll contribute less and less to the winners' positions.

> *Active retailing is actively understanding where shoppers are headed and actively making sure that they run into the product(s) they need and you want to sell.*

Retailers and Manufacturers: Why the Long Tail Is Wagging the Dog

The fact that in-store behavior has been largely ignored is not an accident. The structure of the industry means that there is more incentive for retailers and brand owners to look elsewhere. A large share of retailer profit comes from the manufacturers in the form of rebates, slotting fees, and other promotional allowances. U.S. supermarkets derive their profits from four principal sources, listed here from the largest and most important to the smallest and least important:

1. Trade and promotional allowances from the brand suppliers. (Money manufacturers pay to get their products into the store.)

2. Float on cash (accruing interest on cash from sales).

3. Real estate (the appreciating value of property).

4. Margin on sales (often on high-margin departments around the perimeter).

Shoppers only play a role in the fourth source. When these sources of profit, and the inherent nature of self-service, or passive retailing, are made clear, it is not surprising that retailers don't know a lot about the actual behavior of the shoppers in their stores. Why should they? The shoppers have been assigned responsibility for their own shopping and aren't really complaining. This business model may be inefficient, but it is not irrational. (Las Vegas also is inefficient, except in relieving gamblers of their money, but nobody is predicting that Vegas will disappear any time soon.) The retailers are paid by manufacturers to stock many SKUs (the long tail) on their shelves. But if these products are not selling, it is not helping the retailers or manufacturers. The long tail is wagging the dog. Although the long tail can attract customers to the store—because they know they can find whatever they need—it can impede shopping in the store if not carefully managed, reducing sales.

The relationship between retailers and brand suppliers is changing. In the age of mass media, major brand manufacturers dominated retailing. The brands "had their way" with the market. Now, the power has shifted more to retailers, thanks in part to Sam Walton, who made Wal-Mart the largest corporation in the world. Today, the adage: "The brands have all the money, but the retailers have all the power" is at least partly true. The nonautomotive retailing business is a $14 trillion business, globally. Of this, the brands get $8 trillion, while the retailers get $6 trillion. But there are no absolutes. Although retailers *can* forgo major brands, few take that approach. Ol' Roy may be the top-selling dog food brand, but Wal-Mart still sells a lot of other-branded dog food. And remember, even Wal-Mart has highly successful competitors, using other business models.

In Chapter 5, "Brands, Retailers, and Shoppers: Why the Long Tail Is Wagging the Dog," we consider how retailers and brand owners can work together more effectively to manage "flow and adjacency." If shoppers do not buy products in stores, no one wins. This is a compelling reason for the two sides of retailing to work more closely together.

Rapid Change: Online, Multicultural, and Industry Insights

The world of retailing is changing so rapidly that even researchers with cameras and RFID tags on millions of shopper trips cannot gain the full picture. In the second part of the book, we interview a set of experts who offer additional insights on the forces changing retailing. In Chapter 6, "The Quick-Trip Paradox," Mike Twitty of Unilever looks at the quick trip in more detail. In particular, he points out what he calls the "Quick-Trip Paradox": Although most shoppers come to the store on quick trips, the types of products they buy are all over the map, so it is hard to create a "quick trip" selection of products.

While many observers feel that online and offline retailing have little in common, Professors Peter Fader of The Wharton School and Wendy Moe of the University of Maryland note that there are many things that bricks-and-clicks retailers can learn from one another. They explore the insights and opportunities from their research on shopping online and in stores in Chapter 7, "Integrating Online and Offline Retailing." With new in-store technologies, the lines between these two worlds are increasingly beginning to blur. In Chapter 8, "Multicultural Retailing," Emil Morales of TNS Multicultural explores the rise of the U.S. Hispanic market and the implications for multicultural retailing around the globe. In particular, immigrants from developing countries are used to small stores with traditional active retailing, so retailers need to address both the ethnic culture and the shopping culture of these segments. Finally, Mark Heckman of Marsh Supermarkets offers closing perspectives in Chapter 9, "Insights into Action: A Retailer Responds," on the ideas in this book, from the perspective of applying these concepts where cart meets the aisle. The conclusion of the book then examines some of the emerging technologies that are continuing to transform the retailing experience.

Shopping Serengeti

The food industry is the world's largest industry—the African Serengeti of our modern consumer society, an ecosystem teeming with life and activity. You can look at shoppers in a more constrained environment—which makes research much easier. For example, television and online interactions are passive and uni-directional. The viewer looks in one direction and you know what they are seeing (although you also can track where they look on a web page). Shopping, in contrast, is complex and multidirectional. Shoppers are moving through the environment, changing their gaze, and taking an active role in directing the experience.

The shopping environment is much more challenging to study but offers much more meaningful insights into shopper behavior. Unlike television and the computer, the in-store experience is 360-degrees, 3D, and in living color. It also passes by at blazing speeds. Although researchers may study brand impressions in the laboratory of 30 seconds, if you use eye-tracking technology to see what shoppers see at the point of purchase, it may actually take them only three seconds to decide on a purchase. This fast-paced, sensory-rich interaction also might be what makes the shopping experience so attractive to customers, leading to the surprising endurance of in-store shopping when there are much more efficient virtual alternatives. (Remember when WebVan was going to replace bricks-and-mortar stores?) To understand what shoppers truly care about, you have to spend some time with them walking through the store. It is very hard to understand how to influence behavior in this environment, but we have proven that you can use an understanding of shoppers to increase sales and profits.

In the past decade, there has been tremendous growth in recognition of the value of transaction data associated with specific shoppers through shopper loyalty cards. In fact, what was at the time a very small consultancy, Dunnhumby, assisted Tesco's move up to the position of third-largest retailer globally, by looking at the purchases of individual shoppers, linked to demographics and other characteristics. But these, and other measures such as customer satisfaction, are output measures. They still don't tell us about the process that customers use to shop in the store.

As with the shopper in the Stop & Shop, we know exactly where and how shoppers walked, how fast and how far, where they stopped, where they lingered, and when and where they actually selected an item for purchase, including whether that was in the main category aisle or at a secondary display. We also know how that behavior related to other shoppers, both at the same time and spread over weeks and months.

Understanding how shoppers shop can lead to better designs and strategies that can significantly boost sales and profits. Although we live in a world of Smart Carts and new high-tech approaches, many of which are quite valuable, the insights in this book don't require fancy technology to implement. It took sophisticated technology to generate this knowledge, but implementing it requires primarily a shift from a passive to an active mindset. The greatest obstacle to this shift in thinking, in the words of Daniel Boorstin, is the "illusion of knowledge." We think we understand what shoppers do in the store. But there are many misconceptions, even by relatively sophisticated retailers and manufacturers. This book offers research-driven insights that can challenge these illusions and shift our thinking, so we can better understand the brave new world of active retailing. This shift in mindset is the true revolution and greatest opportunity in retailing.

Endnotes

1. Of course, some may disagree with this more narrow definition of shoppers as strictly in store, extending their focus to the preshopping experience, as we will see in the interview with Unilever's Mike Twitty in Chapter 6. While this is not to discount the influence of factors outside the store, I believe the dynamics of in-store behavior are so compelling that they shape the shopping experience.

2. Jeffrey S. Larson, Eric T. Bradlaw, and Peter S. Fader, "An Exploratory Look at Supermarket Shopping Paths," *International Journal of Research in Marketing*, 22 (2005), 395-414.

PART I

Active Retailing

1

The Quick Trip: Eighty Percent of Shopper Time Is Wasted

"I am the world's worst salesman; therefore I must make it easy for people to buy."

—Frank W. Woolworth

In the fall of 2008, Wal-Mart launched a set of small stores in Phoenix, Arizona.[1] With the arrival of these "Marketside" stores, it was clear that even the king of the mega-store was beginning to think small. The move was apparently in response to the arrival of UK retailer Tesco, which had come to the United States with its "Fresh & Easy" small-format stores. Tesco opened dozens of the stores in Nevada, Arizona, and Southern California. Safeway, Jewel-Osco, and many others are downsizing stores in an attempt to upsize profits. Retailers such as Trader Joe's and other specialty stores have also successfully pursued the smaller store model in the age of mega-stores. When Wal-Mart is building smaller stores, it is clear that there is a shift in the winds. At the heart of this change, and the success of these smaller formats, is the quick-trip shopper.

Across the pond, German discounters Lidl and Aldi are growing rapidly in the British market with stores that are a tenth the size of Tesco or Asda stores. The smaller stores offer a faster trip with a more limited selection at lower prices. Although large UK superstores typically stock 32,000 different items, so shoppers are likely to find any obscure product they need to stock their pantries, Lidl carries 1,600 SKUs and an Aldi store sells just 900 items.[2] Aldi, which arrived in the United States in 1976, has more than 1,000 stores. It is rapidly expanding its U.S. presence and competing aggressively against Wal-Mart and Kroger's, using a limited selection and lower prices, as well as very different store designs.[3]

The rapid growth of Lidl and Aldi was aided by a tough economy in 2008, which sent more shoppers looking for discounts. But their success also depends upon an understanding of the power of the quick trip. Most supermarkets are designed for shoppers who are stocking up their pantries, but most shoppers walk out of the store with only a few items. In fact, the most common number of items purchased in a supermarket is *one!*

Three Shoppers: Quick Trip, Fill-In, and Stock-Up

Building on the work of Wharton Professor Peter Fader, we studied data collected on 75,000 shoppers across a series of three stores to develop behavioral segmentation of shoppers. By mathematically clustering a large number of shoppers by factors such as how fast they walk, how fast they spend money, how much of the store they visit, and how long their trips are, we found that shoppers group themselves into three basic segments or clusters, as shown in Table 1.1.

Table 1.1   Quick-trip shoppers spend more quickly than other segments.[4]

	Clusters - Market Segments		
Description	Quick	Fill-in	Stock-up
Share of store visited	11.2%	21.1%	41.0%
Trip duration (in minutes)	13.4	18.5	25.3
Walking speed (feet per second)	0.52	0.66	0.98
Buy time (seconds to buy a single unit)	38.7	30.2	21
Spending speed (dollars per minute)	$1.88	$1.32	$1.23
Efficiency (seconds per dollar)	31.9	45.5	48.8

Each of the segments exhibits fairly distinctive shopping behavior, as follows:

- **Quick:** Short time, small area, slow walk, high-spending speed, very efficient.

- **Fill-in:** Medium time, medium area, slow walk, average-spending speed, modest efficiency.

- **Stock-up:** Long time, large area, fast walk, low-spending speed, lowest efficiency.

Very few supermarket retailers are aware that half of all shopping trips result in the purchase of five or fewer items (these numbers come from actual transaction logs from every continent except Africa and Antarctica). This ignorance is a consequence of the justified focus on the economics of the stock-up shopper, and a lack of attention to the behavior of the mass of individual shoppers in the store. This huge cohort of quick trippers is not a different breed of shoppers. They are simply stock-up shoppers on a different mission.

Anyway you slice it, these quick trips are an important part of retailing. *Single item* purchases account for more than 16 percent of all shopping trips. Further, as noted, half of all shoppers walk out with five items or less, and the average purchase size is about 12 items. As shown in the figure, in addition to looking at the average, we also need to consider the "median," half of the distribution, and the "mode," the most common result (see the box for discussion).

The Danger of Using "The Average"

It is important to have a good understanding of the problems of using "average" data in many shopping scenarios. When we looked at the distribution of the number of items shoppers purchase on typical trips, we saw that the "average" could be grossly misleading, because *one* is the single most common number of items purchased, while half of all supermarket trips result in purchases of *five* or fewer items—the other half, more, of course—but the arithmetic mean number of items is *twelve*. This is because half of the shoppers buying five or fewer items only constitute about a third of store sales, so the much larger baskets, though fewer in number, skew

---

the share of total store sales. The bottom line is that simply using the arithmetic mean to try to understand shoppers is certain to give an erroneous view. The median (half of the shoppers) and the mode (most) are also important.

Another example that illustrates the problem of averages as applied to shoppers became apparent when we sought to define trip lengths by number of items purchased, rather than by the amount of time spent on the trip. It seemed perfectly logical that shoppers buying fewer items in the store spend less time, and those buying many items would be spending lots of time. This reasoning seemed especially useful based on our earlier efforts to understand how long shoppers spend standing in line at the checkout and elsewhere. For example, it takes a relatively constant 8–10 seconds per item for a shopper to unload her items onto the belt, the checker to scan them, and to get them bagged, *plus* about a constant 90 seconds that is involved in meeting/greeting the checker, handling the payment process, and so on. Of course, this time is all in addition to wait time in the queue, in terms of total checkout time. But the point is, there *is* a relatively constant per item time. So, it would seem likely that a similar relation might exist between total time spent on the sales floor and the number of items purchased.

First, the good news: There is a relation between the number of items purchased and the length of the trip. The bad news is that these are *modes*, not means. That is, they are the most common trip durations for items purchased—but are not the average. For single-item purchasers, rather than the 2 to 5 minutes that might be reasonable, some single-item purchasers stretch this out to 10 or 20 minutes (perhaps waiting for a co-shopper). With each increase in number of items purchased, the distribution begins to broaden. At the dozen "average" number of items purchased, the distribution of trip durations is so broad as to hardly be useful in trying to relate the number of items to the length of the trip. As these examples illustrate, it is important to understand the average, but not get caught in the average quicksand. To understand shopping behavior, we also need to look at the mode and the mean.

But it is not sufficient simply to begin catering to quick trippers. Rather, the store must be distinctly managed for all three types of shoppers, particularly the quick trippers *and* stock-up shoppers. Supermarketers are obsessed with stock-up trips, because even though there are so few of them, each one is worth a lot of money. But this has led to ignoring the importance of the one- to five-item trip. Even though these are smaller baskets, there are so many of them that they still constitute fully one-third of all the store's sales. What is more, they represent a tremendous opportunity. Although it might be hard to convince a stock-up shopper to put another half-dozen items into a bulging cart, the quick tripper may have a hand free or room in a basket if the right product comes into view. Because the one- to five-item basket is presently generating one-third of dollar sales, simply doubling the size of those small baskets would increase total store sales by more than 30 percent.

But this is not simply about figuring out how to coax customers into picking up a few extra items on trips that continue to look just like the ones they are taking now. Instead, there is a need to understand *distinctly* the three primary types of shopping trips: quick trips, fill-in trips, and stock-up shopping. Those retailers and brands that make a conscious and focused distinction between the quick trip and the stock-up trip will steadily pull ahead in sales and profits.

Rise of the Small Store

When supermarkets failed to respond to the needs of half their shopping trips, others stepped into the vacuum. This led to the creation of the entire convenience store industry and encouraged the growth of competitors with small-store formats. In 2007, for the first time in two decades of expanding superstores, the average size of a grocery store fell slightly. It appears that large retailers are finally waking up to the power of the quick trip.

Many of these smaller stores such as Lidl and Aldi attribute their success to their low pricing. But in addition to offering discounts, they have created streamlined stores that reduce navigational and choice angst. Many consumer studies show that pricing is not the primary factor that drives retail. Giving people money to buy things has to be the least creative way of selling something. As with Stew Leonard attributing his success to superior customer service, the success of retailers might not be for the reason they think. In the case of Lidl, Aldi, and others, our studies indicate that the reduction in SKUs and simpler navigation may play as great a role as pricing in their success.

At the same time that supermarkets were being attacked by the small stores from below, the big box outlets were taking a large slice of the stock-up shoppers. Winning retailers of the future will earn their top-tier status through clearly distinguishing shoppers into quick/fill-in versus stock-up, and serving the two groups distinctly, rather than dumping the whole store together and expecting the shoppers to sort it out. This does not mean, however, that it cannot all be done in the same building.

A Slow Walk on a Quick Trip

It seems counter-intuitive that a quick-trip shopper would walk more slowly than a stock-up shopper. But bear in mind that this "walking speed" is an average based on their total shopping trip— total distance walked divided by total time. The trip itself is composed of time shoppers spend actually selecting merchandise for purchase *and* time they spend cruising from one purchase location to another. The greater the share of their time spent purchasing, the slower the average walking speed.

So, quick trippers have very slow average walking speeds due to their high focus on purchasing, whereas stock-up shoppers have very fast average walking speeds due to the high percentage of their time spent navigating around the store, with an occasional purchase. This is the kind of reality of shopping that is totally missed by researchers studying about shopping but not studying the phenomenon itself.

Perils of Promotion

Given the predominance of the quick-trip shopper, how important are traditional promotions? Promotions are designed for stock-up shoppers, not for quick trippers. If shoppers are only buying a handful of items, promotions probably don't have their desired effect in either attracting them to the store or generating sales inside. In fact, in a 1997 study of 300 randomly chosen shoppers in four retail chains, Glen Terbeek found that consumers were unaware that 51 percent of the promoted items they had purchased were on sale; the discount had no impact on their buying behavior.

Of those 49 percent who were aware of the promotion, 40 percent would have bought the item anyway; 37 percent switched from another brand, and only 23 percent purchased product "incremental" to their regular buying behavior. Terbeek's conclusion: "Trade promotion is unproductive, disruptive, and complex, with a dubious return on investment for anyone. Specifically, hidden costs are higher, and benefits much lower, than participants imagine."[5]

The hidden cost of price promotions is also emphasized by Rui Susan Huang and John Dawes in their paper for the Ehrenberg Bass Institute for Marketing Science. Analyzing 3,000 price promotions, they found that the promotions had a hidden cost: the profit margin forsaken on sales that would have been made at the normal price, which they call the "baseline" volume. In many cases, the baseline volume that is sold cheaply is twice as much as the extra sales arising from the price promotion. As they write, "Plainly, many price promotions result in a price reduction on significant amounts of inventory that would have been sold anyway.... This means that marketers are paying a heavy price for making some extra sales from price promotions—for every extra sale, they are often giving away margin on another two times as much volume (or more). So while many marketing people and trade sales teams say 'price promotions work,' these promotions have massive costs in foregone margin on sales that would have been made anyway, at a normal price."[6]

Of course, as we will consider later, the promotions may have more to do with the relationship between the retailer and manufacturer than the retailer and shopper. Even so, they are ostensibly designed to increase sales and seem to be less effective than expected in this task.

The Big Head and Long Tail

Once the behavioral groups are identified, it is important to match the groups to their distinctive purchases. For the segments identified in this study, the share of shoppers who purchase something from each of the listed categories is shown in Table 1.2. In other words, once shoppers "group themselves" by the behavioral measures, we can look at the resulting market segments to see what they bought, as clues to what we should offer to each group.

Table 1.2 Matching Groups to Distinctive Purchases

Market Segments – Purchases			
Category	Quick	Fill-in	Stock-up	Where to Locate
Beverages – Non-alcoholic	30%	30%	33%	Common to All Segments
Breads/Pastries/ Snack Cakes	13%	19%	35%	
Salty Snacks	14%	18%	21%	
Health and Beauty Aids	14%	11%	14%	
General Merchandise	15%	13%	13%	
Candy/Gum/Mints	18%	14%	11%	
Tobacco	11%	8%	4%	
Frozen Foods	4%	23%	47%	Fill-in and Stock-up
Dairy – Refrigerated	1%	20%	70%	
Produce	6%	11%	68%	
Breakfast Food	5%	9%	21%	
Cookies and Crackers	7%	11%	17%	
Alcoholic Beverages	8%	10%	15%	
Meat, Poultry, Seafood – Fresh	0%	5%	47%	Stock-up Only
Baking/Cooking Supplies	2%	8%	28%	
Paper and Plastic Products	2%	8%	25%	
Dressings/ Condiments/ Pickles/Olives	2%	7%	25%	

Market Segments – Purchases				
Category	Quick	Fill-in	Stock-up	Where to Locate
Canned Vegetables	1%	4%	16%	
Soup	0%	4%	15%	Stock-up Only
Prepackaged Deli-Meats/Cheese	1%	4%	15%	

Given most stores' focus on stock-up shoppers, it is not surprising that they are poorly designed for the quick trip. Stock-up and fill-in shoppers are looking for the same products—just expanding the set. We want to focus on, at most, a few thousand items that are needed to satisfy perhaps 90 percent of shopper needs. Moreover, because we will deliver this merchandise to all shoppers very quickly—near the entrance of the store—we expect them to pay for the convenience. So pricing will not be promotional, but rather we will focus on premium brands, quality, and freshness.

This is not how most retailers think. Warehouses typically offer in the neighborhood of one million different items that retailers could offer for sale in their stores. The retailers have wisely selected a mere 30,000–50,000 items to offer in your stores. But the typical customer's household buys only a total of 300 to 400 distinct items in an entire year. And they buy only about half of those on a regular basis. Those items purchased over and over, day in, day out, week in, week out, constitute a really short list. In fact, 80 items may contribute 20 percent of a store's total sales, with milk and bananas typically vying for the top slot at supermarkets (see Figure 1.1). A thousand items contribute half the dollar sales. (The same phenomenon holds for other classes of trade.) As noted here, those few items generating the lion's share of sales are referred to as "the big head," while those thousands of other items—and they do generate significant sales—are referred to as "the long tail."

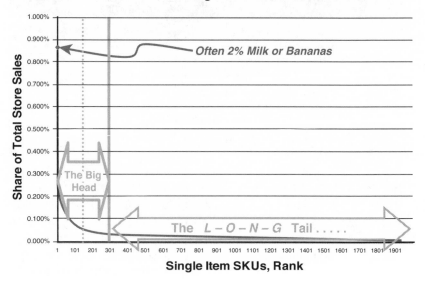

Figure 1.1 Contribution of single items to total store sales

Heads You Win

Winning *always* involves making careful distinctions. There are a few crucial distinctions in retailing that largely define success. This distinction between the big head and the long tail could be the single most important distinction to make in terms of managing the *range* of merchandise that retailers carry. Yet we observe many retailers stirring the two together indiscriminately, in an attempt to sell more of the long tail. Selling more of the long tail is a good idea but not at the expense of penalizing the big head.

Wired magazine editor Chris Anderson has pointed out that online retailing makes the long tail an important business. Online retailers can profitably stock and sell small numbers of niche products rather than only concentrating on the hit products that constitute the largest number of sales. Booksellers such as Amazon can stock an obscure title alongside *The New York Times* bestsellers. The many small sales of these niche titles add up to a large return for the retailer.[7] There is some debate about whether this attractive theory holds true even in the online retail space, as pointed out in a detailed study by Anita Elberse of Harvard Business

School.[8] In bricks-and-mortar stores, however, the case is clear for focusing on the big head.

The reality is that it is easier to increase total sales of the big head than it is to increase sales of the long tail. Focusing on the long tail is equivalent to trying to get more people to shop on Thursday, rather than focusing on how to serve the Saturday crowd better and more efficiently. Slight increases in Saturday performance *per shopper* are worth a good deal more than lots of additional weekday shoppers. In the same way, modest increases in per-item big head sales are worth much more than large long tail sales increases, scattered across the massive range of products. Help your winners to win more and bigger. It will give you the resources to selectively focus on the long tail more appropriately.

Many retailers hide the big head, as shown in Figure 1.2. This is a map showing the exact location of those top 80 items from the big head for this particular store. As expected, there is a significant collection in the produce section—upper right—and in the dairy—upper left. Otherwise, the big head is pretty well scattered about, as the retailer attempts to sell more long tail by "hiding" the big head among those many thousands of items of very limited interest to the shopper.

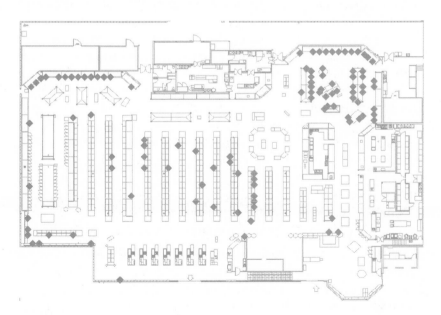

Figure 1.2   Where the big head is hiding

The net result of this is a very large loss in big head sales, coupled with angst, frustration, or ennui on the part of the shopper. Don't worry: There is an important role for the long tail—and there *are* valid justifications for "SKU proliferation," "range growth," and promotional fees to support the long tail—but killing off sales of the big head is not one of them.

In addition to making it harder for shoppers to find "big head" products, a proliferation of SKUs also contributes to the problem of out-of-stock items (stockouts). Increasing from three SKUs to 10 will not necessarily increase sales because it is harder to manage inventory and avoid stockouts. Roughly 8 percent of store sales are lost due to stockouts, and greater variety increases this risk.

The Communal Pantry

The dominance of quick trips means that retailers are functioning as the communal, neighborhood pantry, offering just what the household needs with emphasis on fresh (quality) products at modest prices.

In the developing world, traditional retailing involves mostly very small neighborhood shops where patrons of limited means purchase only what they need "right now." These customers cannot afford to stock a pantry at home, so the neighborhood market becomes a communal pantry. In other words, it creates community. Small, family-owned stores, some as small as closets, provide their customers with needs on a daily basis. For example, in India, about 96 percent of the retail marketplace consists of small shopkeepers. Across emerging markets, an estimated 80 percent of people buy their wares from mom-and-pop stores no bigger than a closet. "Crammed with food and a hodgepodge of household items, these retailers serve as the pantries of the world's consumers for whom both money and space are tight."[9] In Mexico, despite being one of Wal-Mart's most successful markets, high-frequency stores are still regularly visited by almost three-quarters of the population. Although the average spent is only $2.14 a day, the annual sales total reaches a significant $16 billion.

Small stores catering to the quick tripper in developed markets are also serving as a communal pantry. In this case, the shift is not because of a lack of refrigeration or funds but due instead to a change in lifestyle and a shortage of time. Once the home pantry was the communal focus of the home, but now kitchens have often evolved into a fast-food preparation point to adapt to changing habits, with people grazing, or eating on the run. The household pantry is thus becoming de-emphasized because more customers would rather pick up quality, fresh merchandise in the local "bodega" or neighborhood market rather than stock a home pantry, even though they could easily afford to. So, in this way, the modern consumer is returning to a "communal pantry." This, of course, has had a consequential effect on buying patterns and subsequently on storage.

So, this is a phenomenon that affects all strata of society, from the rich to the poor: People are visiting stores very regularly, possibly every day, buying what they want when they need it. The retailer takes on the responsibility for warehousing and stocking the essentials that consumers no longer have the space for or desire to stock, and keeps the products fresh and available. This also leads to the homogenization of rich and poor, who visit stores such as Wal-Mart, Costco, and Fresh & Easy. The objective is to have shoppers come in several times a week to pick up dinner, so these stores are essentially acting as a communal pantry.

A 2007 report by Booz Allen Hamilton notes that, after years of hype about "big box" retailing, there is an increasing number of small-format success stories, ranging from convenience stores to discounters to stores that sell basic staples and key grocery items in a cost-effective neighborhood format.[10] The report cites three reasons for the trend. First, consumer experience in massive retail stores is becoming increasingly unattractive. Lower-income shoppers, in particular, are uncomfortable in large stores because of impersonal service and the sheer number of items on offer, which underlines their lack of spending power. Second, smaller stores are no longer necessarily saddled with higher prices or lesser quality. Finally, small formats give retailers the chance to have a more intimate relationship with customers and employees, which provides scope for genuine innovation in store and business model design.

This is a global phenomenon and is leading to the breaking down of the divide between the developed and developing world in regions such as Europe and Latin America—a democratization of retail. As the Booz Hamilton Allen report notes: "In Europe's affluent economies, consumers are looking for convenience items, including meals, to suit their busy lifestyles of single heads of households. Retailing in Latin America, by contrast, is focused much more on low-income and larger families. Part of the explanation for why smaller formats are working in Latin America is that items such as dry pasta, cooking oils, milk, bath soap, and laundry detergent can be acquired in precisely the right quantities for daily use. The stores are, in effect, the *customers' pantries*. [italics added]"

As these smaller stores have begun to sell high-quality items at low prices, they have come head-to-head with traditional, passive retailers. More important, this shift has tremendous social significance for the countries where implemented, because the product quality has a strong appeal to wealthy customers, whereas the lower pricing appeals to low-income customers. This begins to make retailing a new and valuable community builder. Retail is, once again, at the cutting-edge of social evolution.

Layered Merchandising

Given three emerging features of retailing—the quick trip, big head, and communal pantry—retailers need to rethink how they merchandize their stores. The original idea of the store as a community warehouse needs to be rethought. The importance of quick-trip shoppers argues for a different store design, where the "fill-in" and "stock-up" areas should be considered as extensions of the "quick" convenience area, rather than having the convenience area an afterthought in a store designed for stocking up. Other than representing small selections of the categories specified in the second group (fill-in and stock-up) and the last group (stock-up) in Table 1.2, this convenience area should adhere to the same pricing and selection criteria: high-quality, higher-margin merchandise, delivered more conveniently than that in the long tail. Of course, it is easily possible that the "convenience store" area already is embodied in the promotional store, end-caps, and other promotional displays (see "Managing the Two Stores," in Chapter 3, "In-Store Migration Patterns: Where Shoppers Go and What They Do").

The essential element of this merchandising plan is to offer a common area for all shoppers that serves up the merchandise that all segments include in their baskets; then to provide a secondary area that encompasses the first two segments, a third area for the more extended trips that encompass the third segment, and finally, an "everything else" long tail area where a shopper can find almost anything but may need to spend some time looking. The "quick" area becomes the big head portion of the store, where shoppers can spend more dollars per minute (fewer seconds per dollar) than any other part of the store, while the other areas blend into the long tail.

The fundamental concept here is to address explicitly and distinctly the needs of each group of shoppers as they come through the door. Conceptually, this means that retailers should stand at the door of their stores, call out the first segment, and then ask themselves: How am I delivering *right away* to this group what I know they are going to buy, accepting their cash quickly, and speeding them on their way? The answer to this should be a clear and attractive path that covers all of those items quickly and with clarity—providing just the choices necessary to accomplish the shoppers' purposes.

For each segment that comes through the door, it should seem as if the store was designed just for them. If retailers can stand at the door and know that they are achieving the Holy Grail for the quick-trip segment, they must proceed similarly with the second segment, and then the third. The key is for each segment to sense that the store was designed just for them. And how is this to be done? Through what we call *layered merchandising*.

Layered merchandising simply means that the principal needs of each segment are easily and logically found on as short a path as possible between the entry and the checkout. It creates stores within stores. For instance, say that a five-minute trip, by the nature and number of the items, is required for shoppers to acquire all the items they want or may buy. Remember the treasure hunt on which most retailers send customers in looking for the big head within the store, as shown in Figure 1.3. Treasure hunts might be fun for children's birthday parties, but they are an irritation for a time-pressed shopper.

Yet retailers think that they are cleverly boosting sales and profits by holding the shopper in the store for ten minutes. They should think again. They force the shopper to spend his or her time walking around the store to find items to buy, instead of spending more time buying. Is this frustration worth it just to get the shopper to walk past a few more items? In reality, the shopper is being told, go somewhere else if you want to shop efficiently—here we intend to frustrate you and hinder you to maybe get a little more of your trade. This leads to fragmentation of the channel as needs are met elsewhere. To reverse this baleful trend requires true customer orientation, beginning with understanding the distinctive types of shoppers (segments) coming in the door, and serving each group efficiently through intelligent product placement.

The Right Paths for the Right Shoppers

Layered merchandising allows the retailer to provide *instinctive-distinctive* paths appropriate to each shopper segment. That is, when *all* shoppers arrive in the store, they intuitively recognize, even if subliminally, that all of their most common needs are right around them so that they can efficiently access the "big head" selections from those categories in their pathways to checkout. Some retailers, for example, put a selection of dairy at the entrance instead of forcing quick-trip shoppers to make their way through the entire store to reach the dairy case. The first segment (quick trip) can proceed to the checkout as soon as its members have shopped the common area, whereas the second, the "medium" group (fill-in), needs to pass through and shop a secondary area that should be welcoming and intuitive to them, and again, conveniently on the path to the checkout. The "long" group (stock-up) needs to pass through a third area before passing through the same secondary area as the medium group did, and then to checkout. In every case, the goal is to provide an intuitive, instinctive path, distinctive to the shopper segment, which delivers just what they need from a preselected, high-margin offering, speeding them to the checkout.

The path outlined here would deliver a high volume of sales to shoppers from the 2,000 to 4,000 items they are most interested in, with no compromise of margins. Selective margin reductions are reserved as motivation to entice shoppers to look at more complete selections of the specified twenty categories, plus all other categories, in the long tail portion of the store. But this approach can only be pursued if the retailer recognizes the different segments, understands what they buy, and designs the store accordingly.

There are other motivations/inducements for shoppers to extend their trips beyond the convenient, higher-margin area. One obvious motivation is to benefit from a much wider selection of merchandise. Both price and selection benefits for the long tail can be advertised in the big head portion of the store, without eroding the convenience of the big head experience. Successful execution of such a communication plan will obviously affect the success of the long tail, without compromising the big head. Retailers need to manage not just the big head versus the long tail, but simultaneously offer the long tail to shoppers engaged in big head purchases.

The problem here is somewhat analogous to managing quick trippers at the same time as stock-up shoppers. As noted before, quick trippers *are* stock-up shoppers, just not on a stock-up trip *at the time.* So the challenge is to *predispose* a "soft drink and personal care only" buyer on this trip to return to purchase their laundry detergent or other staples *at this store*. This problem is one of connecting a single shopper's quick trip with the same shopper's later stock-up trip.

Purchase Modes and Selection Paradigm

We also need to recognize that shoppers can be in different purchase modes, and this leads to different selection paradigms. First, the modes can be planned or opportunistic. Some purchases are carefully decided based on shopping lists, research, or careful planning. Others are opportunistic, responding to chance meetings with products in the store.

At the moment of purchase, there are also different types of decision making. Some decisions such as repeat purchases are instinctual, not involving the conscious mind. For these, presenting the shopper with the 100 or so SKUs is the most important factor. Other purchases are decisional, through evaluation and selection, so the use of shopping lists or reminders to buy can help to trigger a decision.

There are also two ways that shoppers view purchases within their trips. The first is that the purchase is mostly not pleasurable or fun, but strictly a chore and should be completed as quickly as possible. The second is a hedonic view, where the purchase is pleasurable, and they might enjoy a leisurely purchasing experience for the item.

Spending Faster

The mismatch between store design and shopper segments, particularly the hiding of big head items in the long tail areas, leads to a great deal of wasted time. How much time is only apparent through careful observation of shoppers. We have found through our research that shoppers spend only 20 percent of their time in-store actually selecting merchandise for purchasing. Because pretty much the sole reason a shopper is in the store is to acquire merchandise, and that pretty well aligns with the retailer's reason-for-being, too, this represents a tremendous failure. This means that 80 percent of the shopper's time is economically nonproductive—largely wasted! This single fact has huge implications, because time is money, and we are obviously wasting a lot of it. (This fact lies at the root of my own focus on seconds per dollar as *the* single most important productivity measure for shopping.) Simply making that nonproductive time productive might give retailers *five times* the sales.

One of the things that gives me confidence in these recommendations is that there are actually multiple streams of evidence coming together that all support the observation that an awful lot of sales are left in the aisles. For example, consider the average walking speed of shoppers on different kinds of trips. Counter-intuitively, quick trippers' average walking speed through the store is much slower than the stock-up shoppers. This is a direct consequence of the fact that all the shopper's time in the store can be divided into two buckets:

1. Now I am standing at the shelf, selecting merchandise for purchase, and *walking* very slowly, if at all (<1 ft/sec.).

2. Then I am looking for the next merchandise that I might be interested in buying, and hurrying along trying to find it, walking quite quickly (1–4 ft/sec.).

So quick trippers have a lot less wasted time than the stock-up shopper, and as a consequence spend their money a lot faster. Remember that *shopper seconds per dollar* is one of the key measures of retailing success, so shoppers spending money more quickly ultimately leads to greater overall store sales. As shown in Figure 1.3, the data show that shoppers spend faster on the shorter trip, as a direct consequence of them doing less walking about and more actual acquiring of merchandise. In contrast, a Wharton School study called "The 'Traveling Salesman' Goes Shopping' " highlights the tremendous inefficiency of the typical long shopping trip.[11]

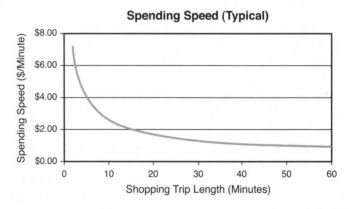

Figure 1.3 Spending speed: Shoppers spend faster the shorter the trip.

As noted in the Introduction, in addition to focusing on the large head, the other massive angst reduction at Stew Leonard's comes from having only one, single aisle, that wends its way through the entire store. This is a wide, serpentine aisle that essentially transports every shopper through the store, introducing them in the same order to all of the merchandise there. This virtually eliminates *navigational angst*. Whereas the typical store is worried about how to get the shopper to the right merchandise—with sales flyers, specials, and flashing lights—Leonard already knows where his shoppers are going and can put the right products in their paths.

For a wide variety of good and valid reasons, everyone is not going to run out and build a "Stew Leonard" kind of store. There are many possible models. The point is not for retailers to copy a simple formula—if everyone is doing it, it becomes less competitive—but to understand the principles that drive extraordinary sales, and leverage those principles in their own operations. In addition to the serpentine design used by Leonard, other effective store designs include the enhanced perimeter, the inverted perimeter, the compound store, and the big head store, as we will explore further in Chapter 3.

Conclusion: Dual Chaos

Matching these diverse segments to a broad set of products—in a way that works for shoppers, retailers, and manufacturers—is a "dual chaos" problem. There are a multitude of types and varieties of people (chaos 1), as well as a multitude of types and varieties of products (chaos 2). The question is how to match the people with the products. In the bricks-and-mortar retailing world, it's not possible (yet) to do an exact one-to-one match. The store cannot be reconfigured to personal tastes every time a shopper walks in the door. As much as retailers might like to customize their stores for every single shopper, this is not operationally practical. So, the best thing a retailer can do is create a "variety" of shopping experiences addressing the distinctive needs of groups of shoppers.

Organizing shoppers into groups is what segmentation or clustering is all about. Although we have considered the three broad segments that have emerged across many retailers, each retailer or store will have more specific insights into how people shop in their stores. There are two general problems of most shopper segmentation. The first is that most of these schemes result in far too many groups of clusters for practical in-store use. Retailers can respond to a small number of large groups inside the store far more intelligently and in a more targeted way than they can to a large number of smaller groups. However, in defense of segmentation schemes producing larger numbers of groups, these may be effective outside the store, where various advertising media may be targeted distinctly to more varied groups.

The second problem is that most segmentation schemes are based on a wide variety of psychographic and demographic data, which although collected by surveys and other research, are not obviously related to in-store behaviors. The goal of the store is to organize the chaos of shoppers into groups and to organize the chaos of products into groups, and then to introduce the appropriate groups of people to the appropriate groups of products. So, in reality, we're interested in grouping the shoppers by their *behavior* in the store rather than by their attitudes, opinions, or even need states.

Generally, such characteristics as age, sex, and others inherent to the individual shopper are subsumed. *Attitude*, of course, is less fixed, but has been given a great deal of consideration in many segmentation schemes. This certainly includes such things as need states and other transitory mental conditions. Although individual characteristics and attitude criteria are of great value in planning outside-the-store communication strategies (advertising), they are more difficult for store management to actually respond to effectively.

Behavior is the critical in-store factor. It is widely recognized that it is more reliable to observe what people do than to ask them what they do. In other words, if behavioral data is available, it will generally be more reliable and relevant than the shoppers' attitudes and memories. After all, in the end, the only thing that matters is whether the shopper buys—a strictly behavioral matter. Alexander "Sandy" Swan of Dr. Pepper/Seven Up, an early supporter of PathTracker™ studies, once told me: "I don't care whether the person buying my product is a 60-year-old man who drives up in an $80,000 BMW, or a 17-year-old pierced teen who arrives with her friends in a beat-up VW. All that matters is that they buy."

Endnotes

1. Andrew Martin, "Miles of Aisles for Milk? Not Here," *The New York Times*, September 10, 2008.

2. "The Rise of Lidl Britain During the Credit Crunch," *The Telegraph*, October 9, 2008.

3. Cecelie Rohwedder and David Kesmodel, "Aldi Looks to U.S. for Growth," *The Wall Street Journal*, January 13, 2009

4. For the more technically minded, arriving at the clusters in Table 1.1 is based on a formula that calculates the discriminants, which are complex combinations of the variables chosen. There are mathematical ways to judge which variables will help to discriminate among the members of the group. Using the variables that show the differences among the clusters most clearly suggests that those are relevant differences. Although any number of discriminants can be computed, you are really looking for the lowest number that still gives a reasonably good description of the data. Those variables that have the most impact can then be used to describe the emerging clusters. A word of warning: The results are based on the variables selected, so they will reflect the analyst's judgment in selecting variables, as well as the available data.

5. Glen A. Terbeek, *Agentry Agenda*, The American Book Company, 1999, pp. 32–34.

6. Rui Susan Huang and John Dawes, *Price Promotions*, Ehrenberg Bass Institute for Marketing Science, 2007, Report 43.

7. Chris Anderson, *The Long Tail: Why the Future of Business Is Selling Less of More*, New York: Hyperion, 2006.

8. Anita Elberse, "Should You Invest in the Long Tail?" *Harvard Business Review*, July-August 2008.

9. "P&G's Global Target: Shelves of Tiny Stores," *The Wall Street Journal*, July 16, 2007.

10. Ripsam, Martinez, Navarro, 2007, Booz Allen Hamilton.

11. "The 'Traveling Salesman' Goes Shopping: The Efficiency of Purchasing Patterns in the Grocery Store" (http://knowledge.wharton.upenn.edu/article.cfm?articleid=1608).

2

Three Moments of Truth and Three Currencies

"If we will not buy, we cannot sell."

—U.S. President William McKinley

A few years ago, Guinness worked with ID Magasin, one of Britain's leading retail research and design companies, to improve its sales. They created in-store displays designed to stop customers and get them to buy. To analyze behavior, researchers filmed thousands of customers visiting the beer, wine, and spirits aisles, and interviewed a large sample afterward. Selected participants wore point-of-focus/eye-mark recorders, which record the precise point-of-focus of the eyes. This provided quantitative data on penetration and conversion rates and the nature and duration of consumer interaction with the category. It also enabled understanding of the search and selection process and established the draw of the various elements of the displays.

Exhaustive analysis of the findings indicated principles to improve in-store visibility. Based on these, Guinness created a prototype fixture and installed it in test stores, as shown in Figure 2.1. The extruding fins were highly visible, ensuring that the offer would reach shoppers at the end of the aisle. The fins also broke the linear nature of the aisle, helping to stop shoppers by the display. Product layout was clear and authoritative. All these elements were within the cone of vision. Strong brand block and the use of signpost products reduced visual "noise," strengthened impact, and acted as guides around the fixture.

Figure 2.1 This Guinness display, using fins to break the aisle, helped stop shoppers and increase sales dramatically.

Guinness monitored checkout scanner data in the test stores. It then modified the design in response to these findings and installed the display in various retail sites. Guinness then installed the new display in ten sites and identified another ten control sites for a formal test.

The new fixture increased sales dramatically. Why? The new display was able to pull customers through the three moments of truth: reaching, stopping, and closing the sale. The fixture made stout easier to find in this busy category, so the display *reached* out to shoppers. The time until the first customer interaction decreased from an average of 38 seconds to 11 seconds. The majority of stout purchasers went straight to the fixture, so it did a better job *stopping* them in front of the display. The total average visit time reduced from 2.08 minutes to 1.53 minutes, indicating that it is easier to shop from the new fixture. U-turning in the middle of the aisle halved, to only 24 percent. More customers were now shopping the whole aisle. And, finally, these customers *bought* Guinness in much higher numbers. In the test stores, Guinness draught sales increased by 25 percent in value and 24 percent in volume. Total stout sales grew by 10 percent and total beer sales by 4 percent.

Moments of Truth

Each shopper second is a moment of truth—an opportunity to sell something. Unfortunately, many of these seconds are lost. As noted in

Chapter 1, "The Quick Trip: Eighty Percent of Shopper Time Is Wasted," in the typical retail store, 80 percent of these seconds are wasted in commuting between shopping points. Shoppers would like to spend more money in retail stores. But as long as retailers approach retailing with the attitude that it is a tussle between the store and the shopper about money, and just how to relieve shoppers of a bit more of it, stores will get only their minimum allowance. Shoppers come into stores with the express purpose of getting stuff they want, and they have no compunction about wanting more. Of course, they would like to spend as little as possible, but that's not because they want to get as little as possible. Focus on delivering what they want, and amazing things can happen. To make a sale, however, retailers need to take shoppers through three moments of truth.

Table 2.1 shows the three moments of truth in the shopping process. As indicated, there are parallels between these three moments of truth and the concept of exposures, impressions, and sales in advertising. The retail experience is similar to an advertising-rich environment. Note that this table includes both shopper "presence" and shopper "vision." This is because the eye has a crucial and parallel role in what happens in the store. Indeed, vision is the immediate motivating force behind shopper behavior, as discussed next.

Table 2.1   The Three Moments of Truth in the Shopping Process

First Moment	Second Moment	Third Moment
Reach	**Stopping/Holding**	**Closing**
Visits (V)	Shops (S)	Purchases (P)
Exposures	Impressions	Sales
Offer	Engagement	Persuasion
Appearance	Attention	Action
Presence	Interaction	Consummation
Place	Time	Money
Navigate	Find	Decide
Location	Scans	Follow Through
Paths and Counts	Observation and Interviewing	Scan Data and Observation

Seeing the Truth: Eyes Are Windows to the Shopper

We shop with our eyes first, so vision is at the center of the three moments of truth, as illustrated in Figure 2.2. There are three general stages of eye activity in shopping. First, the eye serves as the pilot that steers shoppers around the store. Next, it serves as a rapid scanner of a category or section to home in on prime candidates for purchase, and finally it feeds the sales communication to the brain, thereby closing the sale. Just as no sale can occur without the juxtaposition of the merchandise to the shopper, nothing will be bought that does not first fall into the field of vision of the shopper, and it is that field of vision that leads to the shopper coming into juxtaposition with the products.

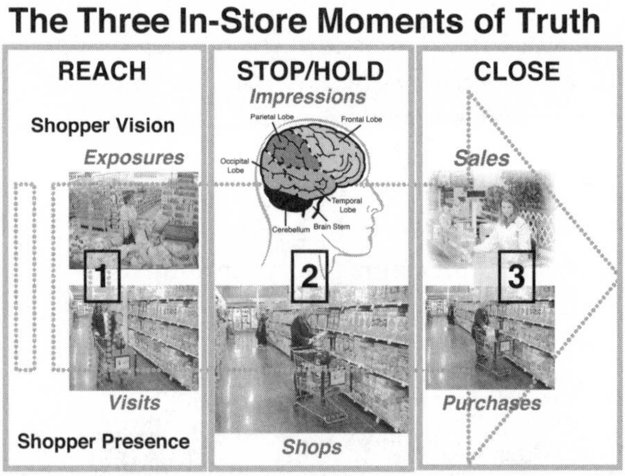

The Three In-Store Moments of Truth

Figure 2.2 The three in-store moments of truth: reach, stop, and close

Vision research offers insights into this process. Distilling what we have learned from two point-of-focus methodologies, mobile and fixed, some general principles emerge that describe the purchase process, as follows:

- It is really fast!

- Category complexity leads to visual blindness.

- If the shopper can't find or see the products, they are unavailable.

- Poor merchandising and communication make it difficult to find products.

- Shoppers navigate using signpost brands.

- Eye-focus level is three to five feet.

- Shoppers rarely do the math in the store; price does *not* register.

- Shoppers have been trained to shop on deal.

- Gondola ends increase sales but the opportunities are rarely maximized—a strong "call to action" is needed.

- Most in-store communication, both promotional and corporate, is not seen by shoppers.

- Shoppers will read very little while shopping, instead responding to colors, shapes, and images.

- Shelf edge is the most powerful location for communication.

Finally, research has shown that shoppers scan horizontally more than vertically (two-thirds of our eye muscles are designed for horizontal movement) and that when standing at a fixture, we work horizontally within a vision cone of about 5 feet (1.5 meters). However, visual attention is drawn by vertical strips when we are traveling (which is why fins such as those used by Guinness work), as this attracts peripheral attention. Most research tests show that horizontal is stronger than vertical blocking unless the vertical blocks are of a sensible width (that is, 3 feet or about 1 meter).

Not everything the shopper sees in the store is for sale. This is a mixed blessing because although shoppers need a break from solid commercial activity, time spent in these areas is definitely not spent shopping. As noted in the Introduction, a typical supermarket that accrues a total of 20 million exposures from all shoppers, per week, averages out to about 300 exposures per item per week across a total of 10,000 to 20,000 shoppers per week in the store.

There is a bigger waste factor, as we have discussed—the time shoppers spend in traveling through the store. This is where vision becomes critical. Shoppers do not wander around the store with closed eyes, and then open them to see where they have arrived. They do not teleport to their new location. The eye leads the body like a pilot. In fact, to understand shopping, it is helpful to think of the shopper as a pair of eyes mounted in a head, with the rest of the body acting as a servant to work the will of the brain. Because 90 percent of the sensory nerves entering the brain come from the eyes, the eyes not only rule the shopping process but also, in reality, rule life.

This has profound implications when trying to understand shopping by measuring bodies around the store. Whereas the body passing through an aisle may come within "reach" of all the categories in the aisle, at any given point the eyes are exposed to only about one-fourth of what is within reach (an elliptical cone, as shown in the left-hand side of Figure 2.3)—unless our shoppers have eyes in the backs of their heads. That is why we always give consideration not just to counting shoppers, but also to taking note of their orientation and direction in the store, as well as the amount of time being spent. Again, at any give time, shoppers have the *potential* for 360-degree orientation, but at any given instant, they only realize about a quarter of that potential.

The right side of Figure 2.3 illustrates the relationship between physical reach and exposure to vision. The parallel dashed lines represent a typical seven-foot-wide store aisle. The six-foot radius sphere (labeled "reach sphere") represents the physical reach of the shopper, whose eye is in the center of these spheres, facing up the dashed-line aisle. Most people's peripheral vision extends to about 180 degrees, but the far edges of that peripheral vision best detect things like color and movement, not detail. The resolution of images occurs more accurately in a 90-degree range centering around the line of sight. For comparative purposes, the 20-foot radius sphere (labeled "vision sphere") is a fairly convenient scanning radius for the eyes. To understand the shopper, we use eye tracking to learn more about the shopper's vision (see the following box). We have analyzed these moments of the sales and purchase process in minute detail, ultimately in fractions of seconds, to understand how quadrillions of shopper seconds add up to $14 trillion of annual retail sales.

How Eye Tracking Works

Eye tracking is an unobtrusive method for measuring what the shopper looks at every tenth of a second. Proprietary software analyzes the focal point information, providing valuable insights into how a shopper navigates a category, responds to POS, or reads packaging.

Here's how it works:

- Eye tracking uses specialist technology to track the cornea of the human eye, thus recording exactly what the eye is looking at (fixating on).

- The technology has been adapted to form a pair of glasses.

- Respondents are recruited to shop a store while wearing the glasses.

- The output includes a recording of shopper fixations (what has been looked at).

- A minimal fixation lasts a tenth of a second. This is the amount of time for the brain to register a single piece of information.

- The average respondent will have around 600 fixations per minute.

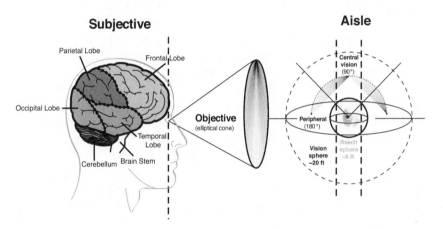

Figure 2.3 Cone of vision: The eyes are exposed to only about one-fourth of the items in the total sphere of vision.

Reach: Impressions and Exposures

Reach is the first essential step in the shopping process: when the shopper and the merchandise are in the same place at the same time. In other words, the product *reaches* the shopper. This is the same process that media mavens go for when they seek *reach and frequency* for their advertising material. (See the box, "In-Store Media," for further comparison of advertising and in-store media.) It is fair to say that no offer to sell has been made simply because both the product and the potential buyer are in the same building.

Everywhere the shopper turns, there are commercial messages—typically packages—competing for attention. Even in a short trip, the shopper is going to be "offered" thousands of different items. The actual selection of an item for purchase, including the shopping part, often requires just a few seconds per item. So, actual shopping and purchasing happens at blazing speed.

In-Store Media

Thinking of shoppers in a store as an "audience" in the traditional media sense can offer some intriguing possibilities. Gross Rating Points (GRPs) are used in advertising to measure reach and frequency, and this is the appropriate convention in-store as well. GRPs combine exposures and frequency, meaning that as much weight was given to showing one advertisement to 100,000 people one time, as was given to showing the same advert to 50,000 people two times. However, in-store, many purchases occur in less than five seconds. We consider both exposures and seconds. For example, even though only about one of five shoppers in a particular store carried the weekly circular with them, their frequent references to it, though brief, accumulated enough exposures to make it one of the forms of media with the highest GRPs. Sales are preceded by exposures. Any exposure that creates an impression that leads to a sale is a worthwhile exposure. Consider that in the typical supermarket, there are a large number of items that sell one or fewer copies *per week!*

It is relatively easy to establish a common opportunity to see (OTS) measurement for all media of a *single type*, because the relationship of actual exposures to opportunities for exposure is likely to be relatively constant within a single media type. However, any distortion is unlikely to be comparable across disparate media: television, radio, print, outdoor, Internet, in-store, and so on. The drive to achieve common metrics across all media must lead to a more careful assessment of actual exposures in each of the media types, as opposed to simply opportunities for exposure. The use of such in-store metrics does create the opportunity to take a broader view of exposures and impressions across diverse types of media.

The point of focus is the prime mover for engagement of the shopper, but the point of focus is *selected* from the entire field of vision, large parts of which never come into specific focus, but are nevertheless received and processed by the brain. And, of course, the point of focus shifts around quite freely as the observer scans and takes note of this or that. We need to make a clear distinction between exposures and impressions. Exposure is what happens in front of the eyes, and an impression is something that goes on in the brain—or to put it more succinctly, exposure is what you *see* and impression is what you *look at*. In that sense, everything in the field of vision is *exposed* to the shopper, but only the point of focus makes an *impression*. This line of thinking is very important when one begins to make a distinction between the shopper's entire field of vision—what they had an opportunity to focus on or were exposed to—versus what the shopper *looked at*—which items actually made an impression.

Beginning with a purchase, we can back up to what the shopper focused on at the exact point when they selected the item for purchase, and back up further than that, asking what they focused on before that, and before that. Once we are thinking this way, and recognize that all those points of focus were selected from the field of vision, it becomes increasingly valuable to ask what did the shopper *not* look at, which *might* have.

Table 2.2 is a direct tabulation of various media that appeared in shoppers' fields of vision in a specific store—without any consideration of the specific points of focus. For the store represented here, we report not only the share of shoppers being reached by each media point, but also the number of seconds the average exposed shopper sees the media during their full shopping trip. Notice that they are *seeing* the media (because it appears in their field of vision), but that does not mean they are looking at it, which would require tracking their point of focus. So, these are *exposures*, not impressions.

This table reveals exactly which visual media (including store staff) are actually being seen by shoppers as they proceed through the full shopping trip. "Reach" is simply the percentage of shoppers who at any point in their trip "see" the designated media by having it appear in their field of vision. For "frequency," we have used the total number of seconds that "reached" shoppers see the media. In terms of measuring impact, the total seconds per shopper are almost certainly a better measure than how many times they see it.

Table 2.2 Shoppers' Exposure to In-Store Visual Media

Stimulus Exposed	Share Exposed	Times/ Trip	Seconds/ Exposure	Seconds/ Shopper	% Reach x Frequency
End aisle displays	100%	15.5	5.8	90.1	90.1
Free-standing product display racks	100%	9.0	4.0	36.3	36.3
Display bins	97%	4.2	3.3	13.9	13.5
Floor ads	91%	2.9	2.4	7.0	6.4
Free-standing ads, cutouts, inflatables	88%	3.8	3.4	13.0	11.5
Pallet of featured product	85%	2.1	4.9	10.6	9.0
Navigational signs (Aisle Directories, Product Markers)	74%	5.7	3.3	19.0	14.0
Shelf ads	62%	4.9	2.5	12.3	7.6
Coupon dispensers/ tear-off pads	50%	3.9	3.0	11.5	5.7
In-store flyers	21%	14.0	5.6	79.0	16.3
Refrigerator/ freezer door ads	21%	4.4	3.8	16.9	3.5
Store staff	6%	1.5	45.0	67.5	4.0
Video or inter-active displays or kiosks	3%	8.0	2.5	20.0	0.6
Shopping cart ads	0%	—	—	—	—

Based on these data, you can see that there are nine different media that are seen by at least half of the shoppers, with the lion's share of that exposure going to end-aisle displays and the free-standing product display racks. Possibly surprising is the impact of the in-store flyer and the staff, both of which get a lot of attention in terms of the total seconds/shopper. For the flyers, even though only one in five shoppers carry them around the store, their frequent, short references to the flyer add up to a lot of exposure. For the staff (not including checkers), few shoppers are exposed, but the staff tend to be in view for a long time—presumably during interactions.

There is no point in thinking about media in the store without considering the package. All media competes with all other media in the store, and not only does the package feature in two of the top three areas of greatest impression—end aisle displays and free-standing product display racks—but also in center-of-store aisles, 80 percent of visual impressions are packaging.

In addition to measuring individual exposures, we can *compute* the probable field of vision from the path that shoppers walk. The head usually faces the same way as the body, and the eyes almost invariably face the same way as the head. It would obviously be more desirable to measure the point of focus and field of vision of shoppers, but the practical reality is that we can measure full-trip points of focus for only a few shoppers in any given study, and can measure the fields of vision for a few hundred. By contrast, we can measure the locations and orientations of tens of thousands and have, in fact, measured the full trips of millions. This means that we can use path and shopper position data to compute reliable estimates of actual exposures.

One practical application of this is determining the relative exposures that every end cap (end-of-aisle display), or other types of displays in the store, receives. Often this analysis is confused with simply counting the shoppers who pass by. But it is so much more than this, taking into account as it does the position and orientation of all the thousands of shoppers who come within eyesight of the display, their distance from the display, and the amount of time they are there. Figure 2.4 shows the exposure all the end caps in this store received. The bigger the circle, the higher the exposure. The end caps at the back of the store (top of diagram) receive little exposure, whereas the largest exposure is at the back of the produce section.

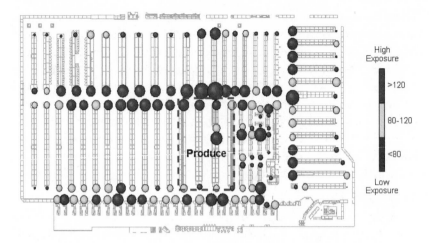

Figure 2.4 Exposures at end caps: End caps at the end of produce receive the most exposure (largest circles).

A study of breakfast cereal purchases illustrates the difference between exposure and impression. The results for nine stores in the study (see Figure 2.5) show that in one store (B), 73 percent of shoppers were exposed to breakfast cereals, the highest exposure rate of any of the nine stores in the sample. Yet only 8 percent of all the shoppers in that store purchased a breakfast cereal, nearly the lowest share across all of the stores. The shoppers in the store saw but did not *look*. They had more exposures but fewer impressions that led to purchases.

Although there is variability from store to store in terms of share of baskets purchasing a given category—cereal, in our example—the reality is that the share of baskets with category purchases is *relatively* constant across stores. In this case, about 9 percent of baskets contain a cereal purchase across this series of stores, across the United States, across chains. To be sure, some sell more and some sell less, *per basket*, but the relative constancy of category sales is a reflection of the constancy of crowds. Although there will be differences, any 100,000 people will behave pretty much as any other 100,000 people will, at least in terms of cereal purchases (and for most other categories, for most of the time).

In Store B, many people were exposed to cereal, but this did not affect the percentage that made purchases. As any magazine advertiser knows, the opportunity to see (OTS), while easier to measure, is quite different from actually seeing. Magazine buyers have the opportunity to see every ad in the issue, but will typically only see a few, and pay attention to ("look at") an even smaller subset. David Polinchock, chairman of Brand Experience Lab, comments about the Wal-MartTV network: While they claim to have 140 million viewers a week in their stores, "What if this study showed that they really only have 2 million *engaged* [italics added] viewers?"[1] There is a big difference between 140 million exposures and 2 million impressions. End-aisle-displays, other free-standing product displays, and the in-store flyers (weekly circulars) receive the most exposure in the store. It is not surprising that 30 percent of all store sales come off end-aisle displays. On the other hand, we have found that even very limited exposures can be highly effective in producing sales.

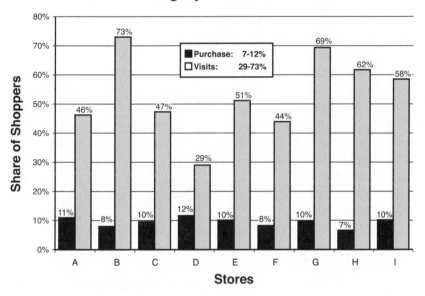

Figure 2.5 Exposures and sales of breakfast cereals for nine stores: Although 73 percent of shoppers were exposed to cereals in Store B, only 8 percent purchased them.

Stopping Power (and Holding Power)

Stopping power is the second crucial element of the process—translating these many exposures into impressions that lead to arresting the shopper's forward movement through the store. It begins with some change in the shopper's behavior. Because shoppers navigate the store by walking around, "shopping" may begin with them starting to walk more slowly, increasing their time within an orbit of products. The initial impact of a category or product causes them to halt their nonshopping behavior (cruising) and switch to shopping mode. It might be a very slight or weak interaction, but it alters the shopper's behavior.

Admittedly, the line between reach and stopping can be hazy. At what point does a person go from being exposed to something, to being engaged with it? If you want to decide this from a scientific, analytic point of view—which we do—then *time* is what distinguishes visiting from shopping, because if you take a visit and add time, you have shopping. Time converts a visit to a shop, whatever other behavior may occur. Looked at from the point of view of the product, stopping power is what converts a "visitor" to a "shopper."

This transition is again a matter of degree. Stopping can mean a "California stop," as when motorists roll through stop signs slowly, or a full stop. A momentary pause may indicate that some element of "shopping" has occurred. But is a momentary pause adequate? Before addressing that question, let us recognize that measuring the amount of the time involved here is measuring "holding power." As in *Goldilocks and the Three Bears*, too much holding power is not good, and likewise for too little. It needs to be "just right." We can also divide holding power into two subcategories: "buy time," which is the holding power, however long that may be, which results in purchase, and "dwell time," which includes the time that both purchasers and nonpurchasers spend on the products, display, or category.

Closing Power

Capturing the shopper's time is only effective inasmuch as it leads to *closing power*. Holding a shopper at a product is a mixed blessing because reach and stopping power, if they don't lead to a sale (or display closing power), become a wasted exercise. Excessive time that does not lead to a sale probably creates angst and burns through shopper time in the store, resulting in lower profitability. The third moment of truth is closing the sale.

In this context, the array of choices presented to shoppers is critical. The typical retailers have no conception of what it costs them in lost opportunity when they jam up their stores with tens of thousands of "choices" that are largely irrelevant to their shoppers. Stew Leonard's chain, as noted in the Introduction, cuts the Gordian knot by eliminating all but

2,000 items in his supersized store. That may seem radical, but it is eminently reasonable from the shopper's perspective. Remember, the shopper is only going to buy up to 400 different items in an entire year. This means that Stew Leonard is giving the typical shopper, on average, *five options for every item they buy*. This represents a massive reduction in selection angst for the shopper.

For some people, this selection angst may not be too large of an issue. But as Swarthmore College professor Barry Schwartz points out in his book, *The Paradox of Choice*, there are two kinds of people—optimizers and satisficers. *Satisficers* have some level of performance that they require when they make a choice, and as long as the product meets their expectation, they are satisfied, without spending a lot of time worrying about whether something else might be better.

Optimizers, on the other hand, always want to make the best choice. Giving them lots of choices can overwhelm their decision system and lead them to either not make a decision, or fret with dissatisfaction over whatever decision they have made, on the grounds that, with all these choices, there must have been a better option. This is not theoretical: Shoppers have been shown, under parallel test conditions, to buy ten times more from a limited selection than from a large variety. Dr. Schwartz describes an experiment involving product demonstrations at matched stores: "In one condition of the study, 6 varieties of the jam were available for tasting. In another, 24 varieties were available. In either case, the entire set of 24 varieties was available for purchase. The large array of jams attracted more people to the table than the small array, though in both cases, people tasted about the same number of jams on average. When it came to buying, however, a huge difference became evident. Thirty percent of the people exposed to the small array of jams actually bought a jar; only 3 percent of those exposed to the large array of jams did so."[2]

As Dr. Schwartz observes, "A large array of options may discourage consumers because it forces an increase in the effort that goes into making a decision. So consumers decide not to decide, and don't buy the product." In this case, fewer choices led to ten times as much purchase! This surprising result confirms what we have seen in the aisles of store after store: Fewer choices lead to higher sales. A passive retailer simply waits for each of these moments of truth to happen, whereas the active retailer understands all three and works with the shopper to expedite them. While the abundance of the long tail may attract customers to the store, this experiment demonstrates how the presence of the long tail in the aisle may impede sales. The retailer that can identify the right six products to sell, rather than burying them in the entire set of 24, can sell significantly more of the products.

Three Currencies of Shopping: Money, Time, and Angst

So far, we have focused primarily on shopper time in examining these moments of truth. But shoppers are not just expending time; they are also expending money and angst as they move through the retail store. Money, time, and angst are the inputs that shoppers invest in shopping. There are two outputs: purchases and satisfaction. At any point in this journey, the shopper is balancing the inputs and outputs. Effective retailing means minimizing the inputs to generate higher outputs.

Most retailers focus a great deal of attention on the money part of this equation, ignoring the other two currencies. Many observers see the retail transaction as, simply, the shopper gives money and receives a product. Given this view, it is not surprising how retailers used the data from electronic checkout scanners in the 1970s, which opened the way for massive and relatively accurate measurement of the money and items exchanged, the two most obvious of the shopper's inputs/outputs. In fact, two of the largest research organizations in the world, IRI and Nielsen, are founded on the business of compiling the counts of these two variables and metering them out to both retailers and suppliers, for a healthy stream of profits.

For many years, great numbers of retailers used scanner data for little more than totaling up the shopper's payment at the checkout and for inventory control: monitoring the flow of goods through the store. It is especially significant that this data is summed up at the store level and compiled *on a weekly basis*. Weekly totals are hardly the kind of detail that might be required in terms of understanding actual shopper behavior in the store.

To understand the moments of truth, we need to look beyond collective data to the individual experience of a single shopper. Individual data for this purpose does not even exist in the weekly roll-ups that are provided by Nielsen and IRI. It is not just shopper identity that is required, but also the detailed log of those shoppers' every single shopping trip and every single item purchased on those trips, which delivers the value. (Better to have all the detailed data for a few shoppers, than all the *pooled* data for *all* shoppers.)

Although some stores are measuring customer satisfaction through surveys outside the store, this recalled experience does not always equate with the actual experience in the store.

Because we know quite a bit about the money side of this equation, we will focus on insights about time and angst.

Time

Think about it: If you are a supplier who wants to move merchandise through a retail establishment, it is not having shoppers in the store that brings you sales; it is having shoppers in the aisle or location where *your* merchandise is. More than this, it is not the shoppers who are hurrying past your location on their way to somewhere else, but shoppers who are spending at least a modicum of time considering your (and your competitors') offerings. *Traffic in itself never buys anything; it is traffic investing time that becomes shopping.*

Time is an opportunity to sell, but not a sale in and of itself. As we saw in the previous example of breakfast cereals, there is a difference between time spent moving around and looking versus time spent buying. Based on a variety of research studies, it is apparent that it takes about a second for a shopper to actually take note of a stimulus, whether of a package, a product display, or some other media. This means that one second of one shopper's time is a pretty good basis for measuring how much shopping is going on. Hence, as noted earlier, shopper-seconds are the basic unit of shopping. Retailers commonly compute the turnover of cash per square foot or meter. This is certainly a useful and valid measure of the productivity of the real estate. Why wouldn't we want something to tell us the productivity of their use of an asset of far greater value: the shoppers' time? In fact, it is not too great a stretch to say that many retailers know a good deal more about the management of real estate (and inventory) than they do about the management of shoppers. One can succeed in retailing with this situation because it is *self*-service, and shoppers are expected to manage their own shopping experience.

To become actively engaged with the shopper, it is necessary to understand how shoppers are spending their time in the store—or, perhaps more accurately, understand *where* shoppers are spending their time in the store. The reason for this is so that, rather than waiting passively for shoppers to find their way to the merchandise they need, we can actively understand their needs and make relevant offers to them to expedite their purchases.

This is a crucial concept. Instead of frustrating shoppers by trying to "build basket size" by holding them in the store longer and hoping they will buy something more, we will build basket size by getting more merchandise into their baskets more quickly. The simple fact is that, in the long run, holding them in the store longer will mean that they won't be coming here so often. Because, in the long run, whether they put words to it, they will come to realize that *you* are not being as helpful as your competition.

But there is a very important point to add: Most shopper behavior is *not* driven by the location or arrangement of merchandise! In fact, a very large share of shopper behavior in the store is not driven by the merchandise. As we noted before, only a minority of the shopper's time is actually spent in the direct acquisition of merchandise. The role of active retailing is to identify this noneconomically productive time and to do more selling during that time. Simply attempting to increase shopper time in the store has counter-productively led to fewer shopping trips, of shorter duration.

Another way to look at this is that, instead of trying to lure shoppers to where they are not, learn where they are (and where they are going) and merchandise to that, as we will discuss further in Chapter 3, "In-Store Migration Patterns: Where Shoppers Go and What They Do." But, of course, this active retailing will begin with knowledge of just where the shoppers are spending their time. It is shopper knowledge rather than product knowledge, the latter being the specialty of most retailers and their suppliers.

The Versatility of Time as a Measure

We have noted that time is one of the three currencies of shopping, second only to money in terms of importance. We also say that time is the proper metric of shopping. It does, however, play an even greater role than simply counting the seconds a shopper spends in this or that activity, including the full trip. In fact, a good deal of our in-depth knowledge of shoppers derives from connecting precise *clock time* with just a few other data inputs: the exact geographic location (*xy*) of the shopper, the exact location (*xyz*) of every product in the store, and the list of exactly what the shopper purchased (T-logs.) Some of the distinct uses of time include the following:

- **Elapsed time:** This is used to assess the magnitude of the shoppers' involvement, whether from the trip length (for the full store), or any portion of the store (department, category, brand, or single items). The elapsed time can be evaluated for all shoppers, for some specific group (such as purchasers versus non-purchasers), or for individual shoppers.

- **Serial time:** In what order did events occur? This should begin with the shoppers' path, its progression, and the location where any designated event occurs. Once all shoppers' trips are catalogued, the trip progression—the first 20 percent of the trip, for example—can be examined for individual shoppers or grouped by cohort.

- **Clock-calendar time:** This is the basic time stamp that is placed on every event or series of events. Events can then be related by identity, location, and time. For example, the items purchased on a trip can be identified by the exact time that trip passed through exactly which checkout lane, and exactly which products were scanned at checkout. This time is also the key to analysis by hour, day-part, day of week, week, month, and so on.

- **Time-derived measures:** Dividing the distance between two points in the shopping trip by the elapsed time between those two points gives the *speed* of the shopper. Derived measures like this can give important insight into whether the shopper is dawdling, engaged, or just speeding by displays. Other insightful measures, like seconds per dollar spent, measure the efficiency of the shopping trip, and indeed, of the entire store, chain, channel, country, and so on.

Angst: A Vague and Unpleasant Emotion

Angst is driven by time and money, but it also arises from excess choice or difficulty in navigating the store. The third currency of shopping is easy to understand but difficult to measure. Shopper's angst is a psychic, emotional deficit that can involve anything from a long checkout line to an out-of-stock item. Although it may be difficult to measure, this does not mean that the effects are slight or inconsequential. While angst is clearly affected by time and money, here we want to focus on two other major drivers of angst, both of which are related to the matter of choice. As noted previously, a smaller selection of products sometimes can actually *increase* purchases, primarily because a smaller set reduces the angst involved in the purchase decision.

Retailers are driving sales to new heights by moderating choice angst, offering a more limited selection of items. But there is a related angst issue in most stores: "Where is the ...?" We refer to this as *navigational* angst. And there is no question that navigation can create significant frustration, whether it is navigating the shelf visually or finding one's way around the store. There are at least five ways to reduce navigational angst, as follows:

- Design the store and lay out the merchandise in a logical and intuitive way.

- Provide signage or other navigational aids to assist the shopper.

- Reduce the size of the store to reduce the need for navigation.

- Remove visual barriers so shoppers can see the whole store.

- Eliminate or reduce path options.

The first two of these seem reasonable, but are sometimes violated with a deliberate strategy to cost the shopper time, in hopes of translating that into sales. Making shoppers spend more time looking for merchandise and less time buying is never a good idea. It reduces overall sales for the store and significantly increases navigational angst on the part of the shopper.

A Complex Optimization

In summary, the three currencies that the shopper pays in the store are money, time, and angst. The key to retailer profits—and massive customer satisfaction to go with massive amounts of merchandise bought from the store—is to deliver goods and satisfaction while reducing the expense in time, angst, and money. This is the crux of the matter—what is the optimum? The reality is that money, time, and angst are themselves inter-related, so there is not a single optimum.

This brings us to a criticism of a great deal of shopper and retail research. It is simplistic, depending on data and tools readily at hand; consequently, the focus is on the easy, not the important. Paraphrasing a professor's criticism of a student paper: "The parts of shopping research that are easy are not important, and the parts that are important are not easy." Understanding the money part of the shopping experience and the products sold is as easy as tallying up register receipts and tracking inventory. But understanding other currencies, and how the three moments of truth lead to sales, is a more complicated proposition. We need to observe and study shoppers to understand their true behaviors in the store, where they are experiencing angst from choice or navigation, where they are investing their time, and whether that time is leading to sales. This approach can also help in improving sales forecasts. To understand how they spend their time, we need to understand the difference between time spent in the three moments of truth: reach, stopping, and closing. We can then look for opportunities for encouraging shoppers to spend more time buying and less time getting to the sale. This requires hard data on shopper behavior—each of the moments of truth and the three currencies—but gives us a much more accurate assessment of what is going on in the stores and the strategies that lead to profits.

Endnotes

1. *Advertising Age*, June 12, 2006.

2. Barry Schwartz, *The Paradox of Choice: Why More Is Less*, pp. 19, 20, New York: Harper Perennial, 2005.

3

In-Store Migration Patterns: Where Shoppers Go and What They Do

"There is no path. You make the path when you walk."

—Antonio Machado, poet

An award-winning store in the Philadelphia area was designed with a dual entry—one entrance on the left and one on the right. It was arranged by the designer in such a way as to make the right entry inconvenient to reach, creating what was expected to be a dominant left entry. Customers were expected to move from the parking lot into the left entry and then proceed around the store starting from the left. Of course, shoppers did enter from the left, but this is where the plan broke down. The designer knew a lot about design, given that the store won industry awards, but not as much about shoppers. When the store opened, shoppers were so determined to make a right entry that they entered through the left door, and then crossed the entire front of the store to shop in the natural direction, starting at the right and moving counterclockwise.

Managers deemed this unacceptable shopper behavior, so they positioned several pallet displays to impede efforts to execute a counterclockwise shopping trip. Given these obstacles, they thought shoppers would come to their senses and start from the left. Instead of accepting the flow of the shoppers, the managers tried to change shopping behavior. The managers, of course, were wrong. It was with real sympathy that we observed shoppers struggling to maneuver their carts around these pallets, as determined as salmon swimming upstream. Because this store won awards, it not only reveals a weakness in understanding shoppers by the store itself, but also across the industry.

Retailers who understand the natural migration patterns of shoppers can design stores that fit with shopper behavior, rather than trying to change behavior to fit the store. Sociologist William Whyte reflects this understanding when he writes about the virtues of a good entrance: "A good entrance draws people—not just those who mean to go in, but those who do so out of impulse. It draws them not by forcing a decision, but by making a decision unnecessary." To illustrate, he describes the entrance of Paley Park in Manhattan, which has been cited as one of the finest urban spaces in the United States. "Its attractive paving and trees extend out to the curb. There is no clear line between the park and the street, and because that entry space is so broad, there is a full view of the activity within. Passers-by look at it. Some will pause. Some will move a few steps closer, then a few steps more, and they are in, without having decided to be... Store doorways should be similarly inducing."[1] Contrast this view with the image of store managers throwing obstacles in the path of hapless shoppers.

The experience of many shoppers and many stores shows that changing such basic shopping behavior is like trying to convince a dog not to spin around several times before settling in for a rest. Understanding and aligning with this behavior can lead to higher sales and profits. In fact, one retailer we worked with increased sales by 7 percent simply by moving the left entrance to the store to a more natural position. This is a huge increase in sales just from a better understanding of shoppers, perhaps more valuable to a retailer than a design award.

If You Stock It, They Will Come

Retailers are quite expert at where to locate stores. They put stores at major expressway interchanges and other high-traffic areas. (In fact, it was traffic studies that inspired, in a way, our in-store studies of shopper traffic patterns; see the following box.) Retailers study demographics and traffic patterns to place retail in the path of consumers. Except for Wal-Mart's counterintuitive early strategy, retailers don't locate their stores in the hinterlands hoping that customers will make a pilgrimage. This may work for religion, but few retailers have that kind of draw, even among their most passionate zealots. Retailers take the stores to places where they are likely to find customers.

A Time-Lapse Photograph

PathTracker® began conceptually 40 years ago when I was stretched out on the living room carpet with my kids, looking at a *Time-Life* book that showed a time-lapse photo of night-time automobile traffic passing through an intersection. If people could look at the traffic on a road over time, why not do the same thing in a supermarket? That way of looking at, and thinking about, traffic stayed with me for my first 30 years of studying shoppers in stores, although I had done very limited shopper tracking studies to that point, mostly focusing on observing shoppers at-the-shelf, and interviewing them about their experiences and opinions. I was certainly not the first to study shopper paths. Farley had done shopper tracking in the '60s, the Marsh super-study in the '90s did extensive shopper tracking, and Paco Underhill and Siemon Scammell-Katz both included shopper tracking in their practices. However, when I began serious tracking in 2001, it was with the express goal of generating an electronic stream of behavioral data from the sales floor that might provide helpful understanding of the electronic scan data of sales, recording the final delivery from the store.

PathTracker® is designed to produce massive amounts of shopper data (millions of trips) to match the massive amounts of sales data available. PathTracker® has evolved into a sophisticated tool integrating data about shopper paths (often measured with cart tags and antennas in the store, as illustrated), sales data, product locations in the store, and shopper demographics, psychographics, and attitude data.

Antennae

Cart Tag

Yet when shoppers arrive at the entrance to one of these stores, this logic and science tend to disappear. Retailers may have an entire department dedicated to studying what happens before shoppers arrive, understanding the traffic that will bring shoppers into the store. But the locational focus is lost once the shopper is inside.

One reason for this state of affairs is that retailers and brand suppliers alike believe that the location of the products in the store determines where shoppers will go once they are inside. So, if retailers put the products in certain places, the shoppers will "find" them—a *Field of Dreams* logic: If you stock it, they will come. This is the model that retailers have followed for years. In their minds, the relationship between people and products represents the most important aspect of shopping. This is an illusion of knowledge and is a consequence of being intimately involved with stores without actually *measuring* what shoppers do there.

The traditional view is that people come to the store to buy goods, and travel from one product to another, rationally working their way through their supposed shopping list. As discussed in Chapter 1, "The Quick Trip:

Eighty Percent of Shopper Time Is Wasted," the quick trippers who dominate retail may not even *have* a list. And, as we saw in Chapter 2, "Three Moments of Truth and Three Currencies," exchanging products for money is not the only concern in the shopping experience. Shoppers are spending time and angst along with their money, and they are receiving experience along with hard goods. The approach of letting shoppers find their way to products focuses on the exchange of products for money but does not place a very high value on shopper time or angst. Whereas money is the proper metric of the outcome of shopping, time is the proper metric of the process of *shopping*. Money measures sales, and time measures shopping. So, if shopping is our subject, time is our focus.

A passive retailer relies upon gross measures—sales, margins, inventory, and square feet or meters—which offer a pretty good picture of the relationship of the store's assets to profit. But between the time the shopper walks through the entrance and reaches the checkout, a great deal has happened. In this period, our passive retailer has left the shopper to do all the work in finding products in the store. How has the shopper spent time during this shopping trip? Did the shopper earn a decent return for this time? What kind of debt of angst has the shopper racked up? Could the retailer have reduced this angst and time, while realizing opportunities along the way to make additional sales? The data on shopper time and angst never appear on the retailer's balance sheet, but you can bet they are top of mind, at least in qualitative form, for the shopper.

A more active retailer plans to pursue the sale by making offers to *where the shopper actually is*, including where they are facing, and for how long. The questions are: Where are shoppers to be found in the store? And what is the most efficient way to make offers to them?

Understanding Shopper Behavior

To understand shopper behavior in stores, we need to look at where and how shoppers are spending their time in stores. These measures are similar to the studies of frequency and reach in advertising (see the following box). As with studies of vehicle traffic used to locate stores, looking at traffic volume, speed, and direction, in the store we need to measure where the shoppers are, how long they stay there (in time or speed), and where they are heading. With these measures, we can create distribution maps that show the high-traffic and low-traffic areas of a given store, as illustrated in Figure 3.1 (which we presented in the Introduction). The checkout stands typically are centrally located across the front of the store. For the most part, the retailer has absolute control over only two points in the shoppers' trip—where they enter the store and where they check out and exit. We consider three insights from these studies: the importance of the entrance, shopper direction, and the role of products in dictating shopper traffic.

Shopper Asymmetry

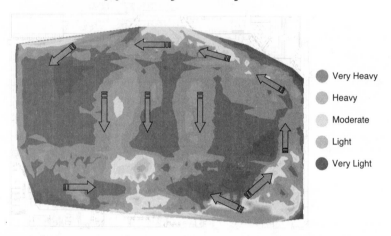

Figure 3.1 Shopper movement through a store

Three Measures: Counting Shoppers, Time, and Direction

Advertisers have long used Reach and Frequency (Gross Rating Points) as a standard metrics for advertising exposure. It was Wharton Professor Peter Fader who first pointed out to us years ago the relationship between the metrics we were developing and advertising metrics. *Frequency* and *time* are closely related. Just as one person viewing a single advertisement five times results in the same five Gross Rating Points (GRPs) that five people seeing the advert once does, so 50 people visiting an aisle for an average of 20 seconds each results in the same 1,000 shopper seconds (Gross Rating Points) that 20 people for 50 seconds would. And just as with advertising's GRPs, it is the total shopper seconds that are the proper accounting of the opportunity of shoppers to buy—or the opportunity to sell, if we take a more active view.

First Impressions: The Entrance

As with stage acting, a strong entrance sets the tone of the entire trip. First, we notice that there are a lot of shopper seconds being invested just inside the entry. This is because nearly 100 percent of shoppers visit this area, and a very large number of them stop at the cart corral to pick up a shopping cart. But this "landing area" plays another role: Here is where shoppers can stop to get their bearings as to where they are going to head and to check their shopping list, if they have one. For the active retailer, *this is an important opportunity to begin the sales process.* For many supermarkets, this opportunity is taken to establish a "fresh, attractive" ambiance by featuring prominently such items as produce, fresh deli, and possibly the in-store bakery.

This, however, definitely doesn't happen in every case. Our purpose here is not to consider the pros and cons of all the different ways of handling the immediate entry, but just to call attention to its extreme importance. And this is *not* simply for grocery operations, but for any type of store. As William Whyte notes in the previous comment, a good entrance finds visitors "in, without having decided to be." Whyte suggests minimizing the demarcation between inside and outside and widening the entrance (extending the welcome) to the extent practical. Personally, I prefer air curtains, even in fairly harsh climates, rather than doors of any kind. It takes shoppers three to four times longer to buy a frozen food item than another grocery item, as we will consider next. This is almost certainly— or at least partially—because of the door that you have to go through to retrieve what you want.

Of course, the second area with a great concentration of shopper seconds is the checkout area. Nearly all shoppers must pass through here, as with the entry. Otherwise, one sees a band of high density of shopper seconds most of the way around the perimeter of the store, with two bands of heavy concentration linking the back of the store with the front of the store. In fact, one or the other of those two bands represents the heavy flow of the traffic from the back of the store to its front.

Some retailers have experimented with left-entry and center-entry stores, in addition to the more traditional right entrance. With center-entry stores, most shoppers turn to the left when they get to the back of the store. The entry is the last place you want to have a choke point. McDonald's realized this years ago when they replaced their small windows for taking orders with a storewide counter. It removed a choke point right at the entry. Center-entrance stores have a choke point at entry. This nearly always leaves such stores with under-shopped areas to the right of the entry. Again, the dominant back to front traffic is the first aisle leading to the checkout, and again in this example, the wide frozen food aisles, which have in this case been arrayed at the beginning of the left third of the store. Almost certainly it is the continuation of the wide perimeter aisle, here returning to the front along the left perimeter, that has encouraged a quite wide distribution of shopper seconds in this store.

For the left-entry store, we previously discussed the Philadelphia store that tried to force customers into the left-side pattern. Some shoppers make their way to the right side of the store so they can move in a counterclockwise pattern. What happens to the others? Some shoppers move directly back from the entrance through produce, as hoped. Others walk along the front of the store and then turn up one of the aisles, then resuming their counterclockwise progression from that point. If they turn up the middle aisle, for example, they will miss half the store on their right.

Shopper Direction: Elephant Herds

In addition to finding out where shoppers spend the most time in the store, we can also discover the general direction of their movement, as shown by the arrows in Figure 3.1. (As with vehicle traffic studies, the direction of travel has a significant impact, as discussed in the Walgreens example in the following box.) We see that not only do the shoppers enter at the right of the store, but that the dominant traffic is around its *perimeter*, in a counterclockwise rotational pattern. This rotational pattern dominates shoppers' movement in the store, and echoes many rotational patterns in nature, such as migration of elephant herds. For shoppers, we know that substantial majorities are right-handed, and a right-handed person, pushing a shopping cart, is going to tend to push with their right hand, giving the cart a natural tendency to turn left; that is, in a counterclockwise direction.

The next question is why is there the heavy traffic through the center of the store, several aisles after the shopper begins crossing the rear of the store? In examining store after store, this phenomenon is often repeated, with the first dominant path from the back of the store to the front being the first aisle where the checkout area can be clearly seen. This is a manifestation of the "checkout magnet," which draws the shoppers toward it, like a vortex.

Walgreens Finds Profits in Two Directions

One of the best-performing Walgreens stores was located on Michigan Avenue, north of The Loop in Chicago. It was on the southbound side of the street, convenient to traffic heading into the city. Walgreens then located a second store right across the street on the northbound side, convenient to traffic leaving the city. The result: two high-performing stores at essentially the same location but addressing traffic going in opposite directions. Similarly, in looking at in-store traffic, to maximize sales, we not only have to consider the volume of traffic going by a certain point but also traffic *direction*.

The second back-to-front dominant aisle is near the end of the checkout area, and through, in this store, the frozen food aisles. But we should also note that it is through the *wide* frozen food aisles. The wideness is significant because "open space attracts." Thus, there are at least three forces driving traffic down this aisle: It is the last visual opportunity to return to the checkout; it is wide and accepting; and it contains frozen food. This third factor—the actual products—probably accounts for the least number of shoppers down this aisle, although the perishability of frozen goods means that shoppers tend to like to buy them at the end of their trip (see the following box).

Shoppers Save Frozen Foods for Last, but Not Produce

It is interesting to compare shopper behavior in buying frozen food and fresh produce. Frozen food exerts a strong force on the order of the trip. That is, no matter where the retailer locates frozen food, it will often be visited near the end of the shopping trip. So, the aisle nearest the entrance of the store will ordinarily be shopped first, followed by the second, third, and so on, across the store. But if frozen food is not placed at the end of the trip in terms of layout, shoppers will often skip it and return near the end of the trip—if they remember—or just skip it altogether.

Compare this to fresh produce. We could theorize that shoppers might prefer to have produce at the end of the trip, to avoid having fragile, crushable fresh produce on the bottom of the cart. We do not, however, see large numbers of shoppers skipping fresh produce, which is often the first category offered to them, although this undoubtedly does occur to an extent.

Of course, progression is not the only factor to consider. In this case, *fresh* produce sets the tone for the store's image, not only from the stand-point of being visually attractive, but also by conveying the message of naturalness and freshness about the entire store. (Having cut-price items prominently at the entrance can similarly convey a *value* message for the entire store.)

We can cite a number of principles seen on this shopper second flow diagram, as follows:

- Trips always start at the entrance, and end at the checkout/exit.

- After pausing at the entrance, shoppers tend to move to the back of the store, especially if that pathway is broad and attractive.

- Once at the back of the store, shoppers will tend to turn to the left, counterclockwise, and immediately begin to exhibit exit behavior.

- The appearance of checkout stands on their left, at the front of the store, will attract many to move there.

- Several extra-wide aisles will hasten the growing rush to exit the store.

Clockwise or Counterclockwise: The Coriolis Effect in Shopping

The pattern of movement in the supermarket is counterclockwise in the United States, but PathTracker® studies in the UK, Australia, and Japan show a much greater tendency for shoppers to move in a clockwise pattern there. This could be due to many factors, including more crowded stores, but it could indicate that while there could be biological or instinctual forces that drive this behavior (such as the dominance of right-handedness), traffic patterns in the store may also be affected by *vehicle* traffic patterns outside. In these small studies, we noted that in countries with right-hand driving, where traffic circles move in a clockwise pattern, shoppers in stores may be more comfortable moving the same direction. Like the Coriolis Effect in physics, where winds and currents tend to veer to the right in the northern hemisphere and to the left in the southern hemisphere, the movement of shoppers in a store may depend, in part, on where in the world you are located.

The Checkout Magnet

It takes less and less time for shoppers to make a selection as their trip progresses. Why is this happening? Shoppers come through the front door with a goal in mind. That goal is the checkout and exit (and beyond), and they behave as if drawn by an irresistible force toward it. The speed of their shopping increases as they near the checkout. The shopping trip is not so much an event, such as a movie or sports contest, as it is a road or pathway (or even a detour) on their way to somewhere else. Within the store, we can refer to this shopping behavior as the "checkout magnet."

The checkout and exit is drawing the shopper away. This may seem obvious because all shopping paths lead to the exit. But it is manifested also in the quickening pace of shopping within sight of an open (and short) checkout line (and by steadily decreasing time spent per item purchased as the shopper moves around the perimeter racetrack). The shopper will hasten to complete any shopping to get into the short line before other shoppers can lengthen the line. Retailers should thus plan for more leisure time at the beginning of a shopping trip.

Products Hardly Ever Dictate Shopper Traffic— Open Space Does

There is a great deal more that could be pointed out for this store, but the single most important thing to learn here is that there is nearly nothing about *products* that is required to explain this shopper traffic. This is radically at variance with very close to 100 percent of all thinking about shopping, which assumes that it is all about the shoppers and their relationships with this or that product or category. After all, people come into stores looking for products. Why wouldn't products be the driver of movement through the store?

> **The location hypothesis:** *85 percent of shoppers' behavior is controlled by the geographic location of the shopper in the store, and only 15 percent of behavior is controlled by product interactions.*

Observations of millions of shopper trips have led to what I call "the location hypothesis": 85 percent of shoppers' behavior is controlled by the geographic location of the shopper in the store, irrespective of what products may be around them, and only 15 percent of behavior is controlled by product interactions. This hypothesis has been confirmed by two groups of independent researchers working to create models that predict shopper patterns across a single store (Wharton) and across multiple stores (Pepsi).

A recent study with Wharton provided additional confirmation of this hypothesis. The study examined the impact of changing locations of products in the center aisles across six matched stores. The results indicated that the product itself had very little impact on sales, while location had a significant impact.[2]

So far, we have discussed how produce and other fresh goods influence the initial shopper landing zone, forming an attraction for shoppers. We also cited the frozen food aisles in relation to channeling traffic back to the front of the store. But there are plenty of examples of shoppers *not* moving through produce to the back of the store, and even largely ignoring the produce if it is not on their natural path. Also, notice that on the frozen food aisles, we cited the *extra-wide* nature of these aisles. Products have a role to play, but they are not the primary driver of traffic patterns.

Open Space Attracts: The Call of the Open Aisle

This is one of the most powerful motivators to shoppers—*open space attracts*. This means that adding a foot or two to the width of any aisle is likely to generate more traffic. Convenience stores generally do a *much* better job of creating open space than do other types of stores, primarily because their fixtures tend to be not as tall. Retailers in larger supermarkets want to entice shoppers down steel canyons, but shoppers like open space and visual freedom. For a convenience store, this extends right on outside the store. If a driver passing a convenience store, particularly at night, can't see into the store, and preferably the *entire* store, they are unlikely to stop and enter. Hence, these stores are typically heavily glassed and lighted, inside and outside.

Drug stores, potentially very effective competitors to convenience stores (they're convenient, given a multitude of locations), could significantly enhance their traffic by getting rid of those fortress exterior walls (reserve that for around the pharmacy in the back corner, if necessary). But it isn't just glass and lighting. I would *never* build a store with fixtures over five feet high in any area where I expected significant traffic. These six-foot and higher displays are overt throwbacks to the retailer as warehouse-man. There is a place for warehouse displays, but not where you want to attract shoppers—you need open space.

Narrow, crowded aisles like packed highways can lead to social pathology, and even "aisle rage." In one incident, two shoppers met in an aisle less than two feet wide. They exchanged words, and as the hapless patron arrived from the aisle to pay for his purchases, the fellow shopper from the narrow-aisle encounter clubbed him. The angry assailant escaped for the moment, but the security camera recorded his criminality. Few shoppers carry matters to such extremes. Rather, they avoid cramped aisles, and probably the stores that have them, in the same way that motorists avoid congested freeways if they can.

Using a few wide aisles as thoroughfares to move the bulk of shoppers around stores is, of course, common everywhere. Beyond those nice "drive aisles," there is a more nuanced question of the "aisleness" of stores. We define this as the extent a store is divided into aisles. There are several ways to approach computation of this measure, but the simplest is probably the percentage of the store occupied by products, fixtures, and staff compared to the remaining total shopping area (where shoppers can actually walk). The higher the aisleness, the more crowded the store.

We first identified the importance of "aisleness" while trying to unravel a puzzle at a chain of gift and card stores. We found that two stores had much higher sales than two similar stores. All the stores stocked the same merchandise and were matched stores, but the key difference was that the two underperformers had much higher aisleness. They were cluttered and hard to navigate. We started looking more closely at this issue across a number of stores and found it was correlated with the success of the store. (It should always be compared across a set of congruent stores.)

The point here is that space in the store is allocated either to the shoppers or to the overall effort to sell to them—products, fixture, and staff.

As the products and fixtures swell, about the only thing the retailer can do is work to highly organize and expand this product space. This results in aisles rather than free space. More open formats—what we typically refer to as a "bazaar" shopping domain, referring to souks and less-structured shopping—are more like typical produce areas in supermarkets.

There are aisles of sorts in these open arrangements, but they do not limit a shopper's walking path. Center-of-store aisles, for example, are highly constrained for the shopper—no turning this way or that way. It is all usually toward the front or toward the back. Of course, those long aisles are often intersected by a transverse aisle about halfway back in the store. This is a highly recommended feature that decreases aisleness to some small extent but adds an extra rank of end-aisle displays.

The bottom line is that stores with a lot of aisleness necessarily have less freedom for the shopper. This doesn't mean that all aisleness is all bad, but it is *mostly* bad, so in general the ideal store will have a minimum of aisleness. Aisleness costs the shopper time, so shoppers penalize the retailer by spending more sluggishly. Looking at shopping efficiency across a series of stores tends to confirm this, as shown in Figure 3.2. As aisles become more crowded (higher aisleness), the time it takes for shoppers to spend a dollar increases. As we have noted, the faster customers spend money, the higher the overall store sales. Aisleness is a significant factor to consider in thinking about store navigation.

If you are a retailer, perhaps you have never thought of actually measuring your store's capital commitment to shoppers' space, instead of to the merchandise space. In fact, it is widely thought that investing in a massive product offering for the shopper is done to cater to their needs. But it is simply not true. Shoppers do *not* prefer to shop in a warehouse. Hence, the slow death of the center-of-store "warehouse."

So, what kind of fixtures should the ideal store have?

- A maximum of 66 inches (2.6 meters) high.

- Not more than 30 feet (9 meters) long, preferably 15 to 20 feet.

- Always pyramidal—sloping back from the shopper.

This does not mean that if you have a store with tight aisles, you have to tear down the store. If you intelligently manage the store, you might blow away competitors. If you have a store with high aisleness and you recognize it, you can intelligently manage it through use of devices such as sloping displays, as we consider next.

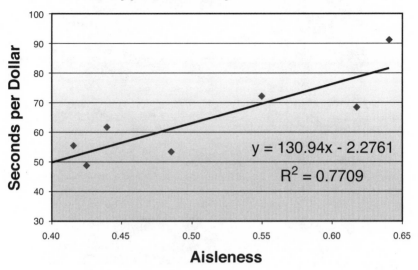

Figure 3.2 The greater the aisleness, the slower shoppers spend their money.

The Great Pyramids

The sloping back is well illustrated by a Pão de Açucar store in São Paulo, Brazil, as shown in Figure 3.3, but we have seen this feature occasionally in Europe, Asia, and North America as well. It creates a sense of greater openness and wider aisles without expanding the actual distance of the aisle at floor level.

We can see the shopper not only has the benefit of being able to see (more or less) over the top of the fixture, creating a great sense of openness, but the top of the fixture is recessed from the shopper by about 16", giving nearly three full feet of *apparent* extra aisle width, if this type of fixture is used on both sides of the aisle. This is of tremendous significance: With pyramid fixtures deployed in the typical seven-foot wide aisle, the shopper would react as if the aisle were nine or ten feet wide. Whether this would make possible a shrinking of total aisle width is uncertain, but it is most certain that shoppers are far less concerned about the crowding of their feet than they are about the crowding of their visual space.

Figure 3.3 Sloping shelves create a sense of greater openness without expanding the aisle width at floor level.

> *The old canard that "eye level is buy level" is quite simply untrue. The true shelf sweet spot is from the waist to the shoulder.*

The old canard that "eye level is buy level" is quite simply untrue. The true shelf sweet spot is from the waist to the shoulder. The pyramidal fixture focuses on this sweet spot, sacrificing nothing in terms of facings, other than above "buy level." The shelf, however, serves as more than a vehicle to *display* merchandise (facings). It is also the primary vehicle for maintaining inventory (avoidance of out-of-stocks). So, the most serious loss is of "warehouse" space behind the facings, particularly at the top shelves. This seems a small price to pay for a greatly enhanced shopping experience.

A slightly less radical design is to use an offset. Rather than a smoothly sloping pyramid, the offset design uses a series of steps to move products away from the shopper. It maintains vertical shelf facing, but at about 40 inches, pushes the upper shelves back eight to 12 inches. This gains up to two feet of the precious visual space per aisle (assuming both sides are similarly treated). This design also allows for the addition of a sloped signboard of eight to 12 inches width, the full length of the fixture.

Some early applications of in-store media, for all their hype, were close to worthless, but new approaches are now sometimes highly effective. The offset fixture may be the true future of in-store digital media, with several targeted messages or "kiosk" functions at perhaps five to eight foot intervals for the length of the fixture. Such deployments, automatically or shopper-activated, allow many of the functions to be found on mobile Internet devices, whether cell phones, PDAs, or custom devices such as Modiv Shopper™ and MediaCart.

New Angles

Before moving on from fixtures, we should consider something about their orientation and layout in stores. Another way to change the customer experience of the store is to shift the angles of the aisles. The angle of the aisles does not have to be from front to back. Rectilinear layout is a clear throw-back to warehouse type thinking. The store shown in Figure 3.4 has aisles set at a 45-degree angle. This means that, among other things, shoppers will ordinarily be approaching these from a less acute angle, which may make them more inviting to enter.

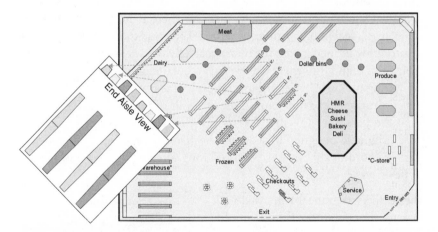

Figure 3.4   Angled displays change the customer experience.

These are shortened gondolas, laid out in a staggered pattern. So, if you are looking down any of those aisles, instead of being treated to a continuous view to the opposite side of the store, you see the end cap of a gondola in the next rank.

Notice also that every other gondola in each rank has been shortened, rather than shortening every gondola. In other words, as a shopper navigates down any of these "aisles," they will see on one side a gondola of standard height, about six feet, and on the other a lower gondola that they can see across, giving them a lateral visual expanse in the neighborhood of 20 feet—two "aisles" plus one gondola width. Also, because many fewer shoppers get to the center of any gondola/aisle, we suggest that giving the gondola a slight diamond shape, or otherwise providing some interruption of the surface of the gondola—vertical signage, for example, or convex shelving protruding into the aisle (referred to as "bump-outs")—is entirely acceptable, and likely to be a plus from the shopper's perspective.

You may notice also the nook nature of some of the perimeter shelving, as well as a designated "warehouse" area on the most remote perimeter. These are ideal locations for long tail displays, and will be discussed further as we look at the five basic ideal store designs.

Many of these ideas are conceived *not* to involve radical departures from existing operations. This is in recognition of the fact that radical changes may be foolish, since what *is*, has considerable merit—including management inertia and shopper familiarity. There is no such thing as an objective "ideal" store, primarily because shoppers themselves have been thoroughly indoctrinated for many years, by the way things are already being done, and thus there is a level of acceptance and expectation by the shopping public. This is an expectation that is not based on strictly scientific, rational grounds but on the grounds of familiarity. (Remember that the persistent QWERTY keyboard that we use on our computers was originally designed to separate mechanical keys that might stick if struck too quickly but has persisted long after the age of mechanical typewriters.)

These facts account for the well nigh worthless results of many surveys asking shoppers how things should be done. For example, in surveys, most shoppers regularly report that they shop "most of the store" on each shopping trip, when in reality less than 2 percent shop as much as three-fourths of the store. There is nothing wrong with asking them, but the results will be a more accurate picture of their current perception than any reasonable plan for evolving the future.

Most shoppers regularly report that they shop "most of the store" on each shopping trip, when in reality less than 2 percent shop as much as three-fourths of the store.

Although we have stressed the wideness of aisles in drawing shoppers to them, products certainly play a role in attracting shoppers and causing them to spend time when they arrive. Frozen foods, as noted, benefit from a broader aisle, but also tend to take longer to purchase—two to three times as many *seconds* as the average item in the store. This is likely due to both the means of display (often behind closed glass doors) and the multiplicity of similar items that make choice difficult. This latter factor evidently also causes longer purchase times for canned soups, yogurt, and baby foods. (And although we generally advocate efficiency in making the best use of shopper time, there are cases such as canned soups where some strategic inefficiency works to the retailer's advantage, as discussed in the Alphabet Soup example in the following box.)

Alphabet Soup: The Power of Inefficiency

Although we've stressed the importance of making the best use of shoppers' time, there is an exception to any rule. Years ago, Campbell's Soup recognized that its soup, with all those little red and white cans with identical labels in many varieties, represented some real challenges for shoppers attempting to find the specific items they wanted. The manufacturer realized that this variety might create significant angst for shoppers. Managers reasonably expected that they might reduce this angst if they could place the soups in a more rational order, so shoppers could quickly find cream of celery or chicken noodle without scanning through the whole selection.

It seemed like a reasonable assumption, so the company created a carefully controlled matched store test, with one test display of soup alphabetized (just like spices are). Sure enough, shoppers could find their targeted variety more readily—reducing angst. This would seem to be a good thing. As discussed in Chapter 2, money, time, and angst are the three currencies of the shopper, so one might expect that reducing angst would lead to higher sales. But Campbell's found that while customers were more efficient, they also bought less soup, presumably because they missed buying impulse varieties they just happened to come across while looking for their target varieties. In this case, making the experience a bit more inefficient proved to be a wise move. There is no substitute for this direct testing with actual shoppers. It is also clear that shoppers are complex creatures. To understand them better, we cannot use simple recipes. We need to use careful observation to study their true behavior.

Having wide frozen food aisles contributes to an accumulation of shopper seconds from the wideness of the aisles, as well from the nature of the product (and display). This illustrates the interplay of the *location hypothesis* with the *product hypothesis*. There is no point in pretending that the products play no role, simply that it is far less significant than generally thought.

Managing the Two Stores

There are two stores inside nearly every store—the main store (primary) and the promotional (secondary) store. These roughly correspond to the big head (promotional) and long tail (main store) we discussed in Chapter 1. Although retailers can't ignore the main store, the success or failure of the store is driven primarily by the promotional side of the store. This is not because the items there are *promotional*. As we have noted, promotions do not do much to drive traffic and sales. Instead, the importance of the promotional store is due to its location. While the main store is located in the center aisles (with the exception of produce, dairy, and meats), the promotional store is on the perimeter, around the entry and the checkout stands or in special displays such as shippers and pallets.

How shoppers are reached in these two stores is illustrated in Figure 3.5. This is actual reach, by categories, measured on a million shopping trips in supermarkets scattered across the U.S. The actual reach in any single supermarket will vary from these averages, possibly significantly, depending on the store's design and layout.

One of the most striking observations here is the minor role of the main store, except for a few categories such as produce and dairy that predominantly appear at a single location, usually on the heavily traveled perimeter of the store. In other words, except for those few categories with large black bars, you could effectively shut down the main store and still reach nearly all the shoppers with the category! Even though the promotional store contains only a small fraction of the total number of items in the store, it delivers something like 40 percent of *all* store sales.

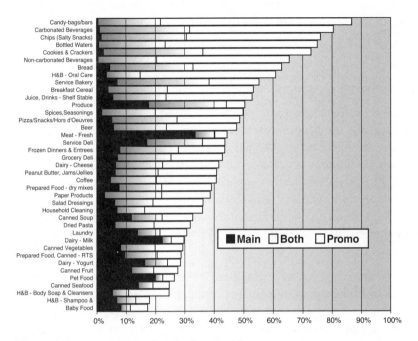

Figure 3.5 How shoppers shop the "two stores"

Take a category such as cookies. Across a wide selection of stores, retailers offer this category to 78 percent of all the shoppers in their stores. They "reach" 30 percent of their shoppers in the main aisle, on the gondola. Virtually all of those main aisle shoppers, however, have been reached by at least one promotional display. This means that the main display adds *nothing* to the reach of cookies. The promotional displays deliver more than twice the total sales of the main aisle—5 percent of store shoppers versus 2 percent for the main aisle.

Scattering displays around the store increases sales. In one store, for example, several of the cookie displays occur in alternate aisles, not in the usual promotional locations. But *any* alternate display, even on an aisle not frequently visited, has more potential to increase incremental sales than another, expanded main aisle gondola location. Of course, the reasonable expectation is that "cookie" shoppers will be found in the cookie aisle. But this is only true in a *very* limited way, since a high percentage of cookie purchases occur outside the main category aisle. Not only that,

---

but we know that a large share of shoppers going down *any* aisle are not particularly interested in the merchandising in that aisle. Instead, they're simply using it to get from one place to another. In other words, they are navigating the store, which is what the shopper spends the majority of time doing. So placing cookies in an unrelated aisle is not necessarily a bad strategy.

Five Store Designs

Given these insights on shopper behavior and movement within stores, what are the implications for store design? There is clearly no one right answer for all occasions. Retailers need to design the best store for their customers and products. But it is useful to think about where the insights into shoppers would lead. A supermarket executive once challenged me to provide him with ten new ideas to increase sales—with the proviso that they needn't *all* be immediately workable. In that spirit, we discuss five models for store design that take advantage of our knowledge of shoppers.

As discussed in Chapter 1, there are three distinct groups of shoppers: quick trip, fill-in, and stock-up. For simplicity, the store designs discussed next take a layered merchandising approach to accommodating two types of trip: a combination of quick/fill-in trips, simply designated as *quick*, and the ever-desirable *stock-up*. Any loss in matching the needs of diverse groups is more than made up by the practicality of execution in the store. For the quick trip, there are a few hundred thousand U.S. stores that specialize *only* in the quick trip—the convenience stores—so I would look there for what is working best, in terms of store design, layout, and merchandising selection and display.

However, some things are crystal clear:

- The quick trip store *must* be near the entrance to permit a quick in and out.

- The merchandise is mostly a *selection* of big head items, not entire categories.

- No promotional pricing is needed—premium and high margin should dominate.

- Visual enticement to the rest of the store should saturate the experience, without being intrusive.

The Enhanced Perimeter

The enhanced perimeter design is pretty much the direction that retailers have evolved the modern supermarket. That is, there is a broad perimeter aisle, which we sometimes refer to as the "racetrack," around the entire store. They have retained the classic center-of-store self-service "warehouse" but have gradually built a very attractive high-volume service belt around it (mixed with self-service, for sure).

There is nothing stunningly creative about this approach, but tens of thousands of very sharp minds have created and refined this structure. It doesn't matter that the reasons for its existence have largely to do with the fact that shoppers need "stuff" and will solve almost any retail "problem" adequately for their own purposes. Another advantage of the enhanced perimeter store as ideal is that it can compete effectively with the other designs we will consider, with less draconian changes to traditional store format. These stores are going to be with us for some time to come and can function at a high level without *revolutionary* changes.

In this format, retailers focus mostly on the profitable (for them) perimeter and cede the center-of-store "warehouse" to the brand supplier—with category management and aisle management being a cooperative effort. The brand suppliers who have successfully escaped the center-of-store dungeon have been the direct-store-delivery (DSD) categories like carbonated soft drinks and, to a lesser extent, the salty snacks. Pulling magazines and candy into the checkout lanes blesses those businesses, too. Otherwise, access to the majority of the store's traffic, for brand suppliers, is limited to end-aisle displays and occasional lobby or other promotions, for which the all-important promotional dollars are required.

The Inverted Perimeter

This store is essentially the enhanced perimeter turned inside out. That is, all of that center-of-store merchandise is moved out of the way, and the perimeter departments migrate into the center of the store. Of course, then the former center-of-store merchandise is properly arrayed, probably still in its "warehouse" fashion, around the perimeter of the store.

Within five miles of my office is a store, based on this design, which regularly does a million dollars of sales *in a single day*! Of course, it is not a supermarket, but a big-box Costco, the highest volume store in the chain, that pushes nearly $300 million per year in sales. There are obviously a lot of factors at play here other than store design. But the center-of-store is a very large open area, with low displays—a bazaar design—similar to other high-producing displays.

Surrounding this are true warehouse shelves, all visible from nearly anywhere in the center-of-store, where the majority of shoppers spend the majority of time. But all that warehouse merchandise is there, just a few steps away, without cramping the shopper's visual space. No wonder sales in a store like this, for an individual shopper, are often double what the shopper intended when they came in. But they like it! Think of all the money they are saving!

In fact, Marsh Supermarkets (the people who introduced electronic grocery scanning to the world) built a store like this a few years ago. This was a remodel from an earlier conventional perimeter store (see Figure 3.6).

Figure 3.6 Inverted perimeter store

Initially, shoppers did not care for this "radical" new design. Nothing in their shopping experience prepared them for such a concept. As time passed, however, shoppers adapted, comfort levels grew, and after several months, the desired sales lift was achieved. The nerve-wracking transitional period has, though, dampened the appetite of management for further digression from shopper expectations. None of this deterred HEB from undertaking a similar approach with its now highly successful Central Market concept. We see validation and a growing body of thinking and data favoring the inverted perimeter style of store.

The Serpentine Design

We mentioned the success of Stew Leonard's serpentine design in the Introduction. Although most supermarkets do $10 to 30 million in annual sales, he is doing $100 million in sales. As discussed, he gains an additional $80 million in sales by significantly pruning shopper choice, reducing choice angst and wasted time, and then streamlines navigational angst by creating a single serpentine path through the store—not to mention his superior customer service. But the serpentine design takes advantage of natural shopping behavior and creates an experience for customers moving through the store that is directed by the retailer. As long as the selection of products and their display are right, then the shopper only has to follow this road and put products in the cart.

The Compound Store

The fourth "ideal" store is less a single store than an aggregation of stores. Of course, one can create a compound store by deliberately aggregating distinct stores. In this sense, the typical shopping mall is a compound store. But what we are referring to here is rather the fact that somewhere between 40,000 and 80,000 square feet (4,000 to 10,000 square meters), stores begin to fragment into substores, which then constitutes a compound store. Below this size, the store is shopped more or less as a unitary whole. That is, even though shoppers typically only shop a small portion of the store (less than 25 percent), they cruise and can see enough of the store to at least have all the square footage as a part of their consideration set. This fragmentation does not require distinct walls demarcating the various stores. Instead, we have found "virtual walls" that divide up the store, defined by shopper behavior.

This means that in a standard supermarket, you can think of the entire population of the store, at any given time, as a single population. However, as the store grows in size, eventually there will be distinct populations in the different virtual substores of the compound store. If there are two substores, few shoppers visit both the stores. One crowd visits one, and another crowd visits the other, with little cross-over. When looking at detailed performance measures, the figures will be distorted because we need to separate out the performance of the two stores.

The Big Head Store

This final store focuses exclusively on the "big head," an approach popularized by retailers such as Trader Joe's and Tesco stores in the U.S.

southwest. Instead of a promotional store and then a main store, this store is just the promotional store. By introducing a 10,000 to 15,000 square foot store, and offering only 3,500 different items, Tesco aims to replace long stock-up trips with many more short and medium-size trips. I think an even smaller store would be adequate to the purpose, and the aisleness is probably higher than it needs to be, depressing shopping efficiency. This, however, is offset by lower gondola fixtures, resulting in the very attractive, greater openness that is common in the convenience store channel.

We note with approval, also, the 45-degree angle of the aisles in Trader Joe's, rather than the less ideal rectilinear, as discussed earlier in the chapter. The much smaller size offsets the navigational issue to a significant extent. I don't know that I would recommend the serpentine path here, but certainly fewer fixtures with better full-store visibility—think Costco—would be helpful. There is no problem with having tall fixtures as small nooks around the perimeter, if there is a desire to include the first few percents of the long tail.

Where the Rubber Meets the Linoleum

Changing store designs requires understanding the big head and long tail, courage in challenging tradition, and specific insights into shoppers measured in the store. Notice that the first two designs I discussed included both the big head and the long tail in their strategy. I don't know how to put this more plainly: Whether brand or retailer, you *will* learn to manage the big head and the long tail distinctly, or enjoy your retirement in the not-distant future.

If your store design is not a result of direct measurement of the shoppers in your stores, it isn't real, unadulterated shopper insight. To my knowledge, there are only three people, and their organizations, in the world who got their insight from studying shoppers in the store, through observation and measurement of various aspects of the overall shopping experience. That would be Paco Underhill of Envirosell, Siemon Scammell-Katz of TNS Magasin, and, immodestly, myself. Like they used to say of EF Hutton, when Paco and Siemon talk, I listen. That doesn't mean we always agree, but at least we are pretty much the only ones drinking from the pool that should matter to you. This doesn't mean that no one else does good valid research. But they don't live on the sales floor—Paco's rubber-soled shoes, if I might. Given the source of our data, we have collectively lived on the selling room floor for upward of 100 years. So I salute my colleagues Paco and Siemon, and the *millions* of our colleagues in the retail and supplier businesses to whom we have dedicated so much of our lives. It is the indomitable spirit of the retailer that delivers to the masses of the world the things they need and must have. It is our goal to help them do it better.

Endnotes

1. William H. Whyte, *City: Rediscovering the Center*, Doubleday, 1988, p. 100.

2. The study was conducted by Wharton student Jacob Suher.

4

Active Retailing: Putting Products into the Path of Shoppers

"Give the lady what she wants."

—Marshall Fields

Early in our traffic studies, we noted an aisle that we thought was receiving very little traffic, considering the number of shoppers passing either end of the aisle. In an effort to rectify this situation and drive traffic to this aisle, we decided to give shoppers a $1.00 coupon for a store-brand purchase of $3.00 or more, just for visiting the aisle. We installed a special coupon and dispenser about halfway down it. Above the dispenser was a flashing red "police light" to attract attention to the free dollars. We also installed a moving LED sign at the entrance to direct shoppers to the coupon dispenser, and on weekends, a greeter at the door called shoppers' attention to the presence of the coupon. In other words, we did everything in our power to attract attention to this aisle.

The net result was an increase from 28 percent of shoppers visiting the aisle to 30 percent in the month of couponing, a 2 percent increase in overall visitation to the aisle, primarily due to more traffic near the back of the aisle. We gave away a dollar off any $3.00 store-brand purchase (limit one per customer per day). This was as if we had dropped dollar bills in the aisle! And still, we only bumped overall visitation to the aisle by 2 percent.

As this example shows, it is very hard to get the crowd to move, even if you pay them. So you probably can't get many more shoppers down your aisle. Does this mean that you cannot influence shopper behavior? Far from it. Take the product to the shopper. That's the approach of the active retailer.

Organization of the products in a store (segmentation) seems so obvious and simple until you actually try to do it. Take juice as an example of a potential category. It is not uncommon for juice to actually fall into five different departments in a supermarket. There will be shelf-stable juices in the dry grocery area, typically in both canned and bottled versions. And then there will be frozen juices in the frozen food department. Chilled juices are in the dairy section, and freshly-squeezed in produce. The organic juices may be in produce, or in a special natural foods section.[1]

Publix, a Miami retailer, put a thin slice of fruit nectar into the middle of an end display of Ocean Spray juices, as shown in Figure 4.1. The fruit nectar bisects the overall display of juices. And, like nectar to a bee, this slice of nectar is designed to attract the attention of shoppers. Nectar is a major draw for the Caribbean customer, which makes up a high concentration of the shoppers in Miami. Once they are drawn to the nectar, they find themselves looking at the broadly popular juices. A minor item is embedded in a major display in a way that stops shoppers and encourages them to buy.

Figure 4.1   Nectar in the middle of the display, a major draw for shoppers in Miami, helps attract shoppers to this juice display.

Placing nectar in the middle of the Ocean Spray juice display not only offers margin opportunities but also *directional navigation* opportunities. Displays like this can make helpful suggestions to the shopper. For example, "For a more complete selection of juices and nectars, visit aisle 8." Technology such as tools to provide map guidance to shoppers for related purchases elsewhere in the store can enhance this ability. (I have, however, never been one to wait for future technological development to do what I can do right now, right here, with existing resources.) For Miami shoppers, with an attraction to nectar, this might be enough to take shoppers to these aisles. The problem in many stores, however, is that product segmentation is often carried out on an operational or other basis that may have little or nothing to do with the purchase process—the ultimate "coin on the counter."

Active Retailing

In the days of the country store, retailers typically interacted directly with their customers, actively assisting them with their selection and purchases. About 100 years ago, the modern supermarket was born, and self-service became the rule rather than the exception. With the advent of the modern supermarket, interaction was no longer necessary, and turning over the process to the shopper reaped tremendous productivity gains.

Supermarkets were enthusiastically welcomed by shoppers, because of their convenient self-service, low prices, and wide selection. Nonetheless, the net result was a large measure of passivity on the part of the retailer. In fact, the supermarket became a neighborhood mini-warehouse, where the retailer stocked the wares, typically neatly on their warehouse shelves, and waited near the exit to collect their payment as shoppers departed with the merchandise. The first such establishment is often credited to King Kullen in New York, in 1930, but was certainly preceded by Ralph's in California.

The wholesale movement to passive retailing created some problems while it solved others. A major and continuing problem is how to organize the merchandise in the store. One early effort to solve this problem actually involved organizing the categories in the store alphabetically. The Alpha Beta stores began doing this as early as 1915, with the chain surviving—without the category organizing principle—until 1988.

Put the Right Products in the Path of Customers

But with increasing competition and higher customer expectations, this passive role is no longer enough. The old store clerk and cracker barrel won't be coming back, but retailers can take a more active role in the way they place products in front of shoppers. As we noted, the traditional view of shoppers is that they will travel great distances, walk through the dark valley of imposing shelving, and undergo unspeakable hardships to find their desired products. In reality, as we have seen in Chapter 3, "In-Store Migration Patterns: Where Shoppers Go and What They Do," there are patterns of movement in the supermarket that are not driven by products as much as by open spaces and natural flows. Some shoppers may come down the frozen food aisle for ice cream, but others just happen to be there because it is a wide and inviting aisle that leads them to the checkout. The question is: Given the natural flows of shoppers, how do you put the right products in front of shoppers? In contrast to the more passive approach of warehousing products for customers, this more active approach might be called "anticipatory retailing." The retailers anticipate the needs of shoppers and meet them.

By understanding shopper segments, moments of truth, and migration patterns through stores, retailers and manufacturers can do a better job of converting visitors to shoppers and shoppers to buyers. This chapter explores how.

Double Conversion™: Converting Visitors to Shoppers to Buyers

For a retailer to make a sale, customers have to undergo two conversions. These conversions occur during the process of reaching, stopping, and holding discussed in Chapter 2, "Three Moments of Truth and Three Currencies." First, customers move from being visitors—tourists moving through the retail landscape—to active shoppers. Second, they move from shopping to buying. Good merchandising will yield high Double-Conversion™—stopping power to arrest shoppers and closing power to convert the shoppers to buyers (see Figure 4.2).

This distinction is important because those two conversions independently measure two different types of issues for the product. In the first instance, it is far more important to know the *share* of total visitors to the store who come within the orbit of the product than the total number of visitors, since the impact of the product occurs only when the visitor is close by and may become a shopper. Once they have been engaged, the next question is whether the product can make the sale, by convincing the shopper to pick it off the shelf and put it into the shopping cart—conversion into a purchaser.

Figure 4.2 Double conversion: Converting visitors to shoppers, then shoppers to buyers

> ### How to Measure Double Conversion™
>
> Double conversion requires three measures: Visits, Shops, and Purchases. Purchases (P) come directly from the retailers' sales logs, or may be visually verified if the shopper is being observed, in person or by video. Visits (V) are measured by all PathTracker™ methods, especially those that track individual shoppers' complete trips, but can also be obtained by directly counting either by observation (personal or video) or through electronic means like aisle counters. Shops (S) are a subset of visits, which we usually identify by counting visitors who exhibit a shopping behavior, most commonly by spending some *time*, not just passing through or visiting.

Various researchers may use different thresholds to define shopping, but it's always the same basic idea of some type of interaction with the merchandise, which could be a weak interaction or a strong interaction. The two conversions are then the share of visitors who become shoppers (S/V) and the share of shoppers who end up buying (P/S).

We now have a framework for analyzing the shopping process. The three stages of the shopping process are reach, stopping power, and closing power, where the critical elements are the conversion from visitors to shoppers, and from shoppers to purchasers. How these three elements are managed in practice defines the difference between active and passive retailing.

Packaging Must Play the Starring Role

Only 45 percent of shoppers use a shopping list. Shoppers are not automatons following out the commands of a preordained list. They are making decisions on-the-fly as they walk through supermarket aisles. This means that packages have an opportunity—a very brief opportunity—to grab the shopper's attention and make a sale.

Many consumer goods companies no longer see packages merely as containers for shipping products, according to a report in the The New York Times. "The shift is mostly because of the rise of the Internet and hundreds of television channels, which mean marketers can no longer count on people seeing their commercials. So they are using their bottles, cans, boxes, and plastic packs to improve sales by attracting the eyes of consumers, who often make most of their shopping decisions at the last minute while standing in front of the store shelves."[2] For example, Evian created a swanlike neck and silver tray for its "palace" bottled water, conveying a sense of luxury. Coors added thermochromatic ink to its label that changes the color of the mountains when the bottle is cold.

The package has to do two things: First, it has to engage the shopper by standing up and waving its arms and saying: Pay attention to me! I'm over here! Second, the package must be compelling enough so that the shopper feels the urge to complete the sales process.

Although everything that goes on outside the store plays a role in shopper choice, the crucial element in the store is the package. In terms of communication, it has the most impact. Far too many marketers view packaging as a labeled container, necessary to deliver the product to the shopper. Such complacency is dangerous, because this is the one factor over which the manufacturer has nearly total control. With more than 5,000 new SKUs on the grocer's shelf every year, existing brands and new products find it more and more difficult to get on the shelf and gain trial. Today, the package is often the pivotal factor in a product's success or failure.

There are a number of reasons packaging is so critical to shopping, as follows:

- For most new products, the store shelf is the first and only opportunity to sell to the consumer. Because of the decline in effectiveness of traditional advertising methods, many consumers are first made aware of a new product after seeing it on a shelf.

- Strong packaging can drive trial and awareness of a brand.

- The package is the last chance to have an impact on purchasing decisions—100 percent of all these are *ultimately* made at the shelf.

- A typical package generates 570 million impressions each year, just by being on store shelves.

- Packaging generates impulse purchases. Research from point-of-purchase trade association POPAI shows that a consumer may enter a grocery store planning to buy 10 items and leave having purchased 20.

- The package is the best way to break through the clutter/noise at retail.

Creating shelf impact helps maximize a brand's chance of success. But more than being noticed is required. A bottle of salad dressing with a hot pink label may have impact, but will consumers buy it? Generally, to improve shelf impact, a package needs to look different than the other items in the category, but attractiveness remains a requirement for closing the sale. The package has to take the customer through both conversions—not merely attract attention, but also close the sale.

Context matters, of course. Brand owners should study the shelf impact of competitors before trying to improve their own. The brand may already be the market leader, but a close eye needs to be kept on private labels and smaller brands seeking to emulate the leaders' appearances. Also, shelf impact is more important in a fragmented category with low brand loyalty, such as barbecue sauce, than in a category with few major players and loyal customers, such as canned soup. Additionally, although the front panel may make the sale at the store, the side or back panel may be more important in the freezer, refrigerator, or pantry.

What Is a Package?

Ten personalities of a package are as follows:

- **Container/transporter:** This is the box, bottle, bag, or can. Functionality is the key.

- **Protector:** Protects the product, the consumer, and the environment.

- **Facilitator:** Is easy for the consumer to use. Easy to open, use, and seal.

- **Attention-getter (shelf impact):** Communicates through color, graphics, or copy to grab the shopper's attention.

- **Communicator:** Communicates brand identity and the product's reason for being.

- **Image builder:** Claims, statements, or banners, which enhance or strengthen the image of the brand.

- **Instructor:** Communicates usage instructions. Can either be copy and/or graphics.

- **Educator:** Information such as fat content, ingredients, calories, and so on.

- **Reminder:** Reminds consumer that it is time to buy again.

- **Secondary life:** Recycling and other secondary uses of the package.

Taken from: Robert E. Stevens, "Creating a Tiebreaker with Packaging," *BrandPackaging*, Fall 1997.

Packaging is the workhorse of today's marketing mix. Not only does it need to be attractive and stand out, but it also needs to do the following:

- Generate awareness through optimizing brand identity, shelf impact, and "findability" on the shelf.

- Generate trial by communicating the product's most persuasive points or "reason for being."

- Support the brand's image by communicating the desired brand-equity elements (such as gourmet, fun, sophisticated, and so on).

- Ensure repeat purchase by delivering value through package functionality.

Having said all this, we emphasize that the first and most important marketing function is to stop the shopper. Unless this happens, nothing more will happen. So, first the product must reach the shoppers, and then stop them. But then it must "hold" them—the intermediate stage between stopping and closing power.

Holding Power—How Long Is Long Enough?

Holding power is about time: How much time is involved in turning a visitor into a shopper? This is a delicate balancing act for the brand owner when it comes to product placement and packaging. Where the product is—both on the shelf and in a particular aisle—and its packaging can have an enormous impact on closing power. Think of a package's *stopping power* as its capability to initiate a conversation with passing shoppers. *Holding power* is its capability to continue the conversation as long as necessary to make the sale. The question then is: What is the right amount of time for this conversation to last? The answer is: Just long enough to complete the sale.

So, the package is the key to stopping, holding, *and* closing power. It is the interaction of these measures for categories and products, along with the reach that is provided at retail, that not only forms the foundation of a systematic approach to product management, but also segues into promotional planning. Location and merchandising in the store are driven by flow and adjacency analysis, linked to the metrics for measuring the conversion of visitors to shoppers, and shoppers to buyers. This is discussed in Chapter 8, "Multicultural Retailing," with promotion planning incorporating elements of the purchase cycle and other consumer behavioral traits.

Before getting into the details of these "final mile" issues, we will look at some intermediate category analysis steps, called VitalQuadrant™ analysis, which will assist in evaluating the inherent properties of various categories, as well as spotlighting potential problems.

Stopping and Closing Power: VitalQuadrant™ Analysis

Because a product's stopping and closing power are the key to making the sale, we can plot both of them in a VitalQuadrant™ analysis, as illustrated in Figure 4.3. It is helpful to group categories in terms of their stopping and closing powers, since entire categories exhibit characteristics that are, more or less, the sum of all the packages in them. So, we look graphically at categories dispersed according to those two measures, stopping and closing power.[3]

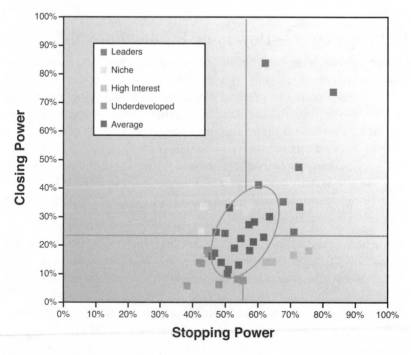

Figure 4.3 VitalQuadrant™ analysis

Beyond the broad average category in the middle, the categories in order of sales performance are as follows:

- **Leaders:** These categories have extraordinary stopping and closing power. If shoppers see these products, they stop and buy them.

- **Niche:** Few stop to shop, but those who do, buy.

- **High interest:** These are window-shopping categories. Shoppers stop to shop, but don't buy.

- **Underdeveloped:** Few stop to shop, and the few who shop don't buy. These categories have little stopping power and even less closing power.

This helps move our focus away from the average group in the middle to what quality guru Joseph Juran called the "vital few." Juran was talking about the 20 percent of defects that lead to 80 percent of quality problems. Focusing on correcting these "vital few" defects leads to tremendous improvements in quality. Similarly, it is clear from our analysis that focusing on the set of "leader" products in the supermarket—as well as the other categories—could have a tremendous impact on overall sales.

Figure 4.4 shows the average reach, stopping power, and closing power numbers for 40 major categories, based on the shopping trips of a million shoppers in stores across the U.S. Note that whereas the closing power overall is 22 percent, the closing power for leader categories such as bread, dairy, soft drinks, and produce is 54 percent. Categories are not always in the same VitalQuadrant™ in each store, but bread, dairy, produce, and soft drinks are often in the leader group. This is a reflection of the fact that they have the highest stopping and closing power of any categories in the store—70% and 45%, respectively.

This doesn't mean that every item in the category exhibits this kind of behavior, but the category as a whole does. However, the type of thinking that goes into this category-level analysis can be applied to subcategories, individual brands, and even specific items. Any category, subcategory, brand, or item that exhibits strong stopping *and* closing power is truly a leader.

Category Conversions by VitalQuadrant™ Groups

	Reach	Stopping	Shops	Closing	Purchases
VitalQuadrant™ Group Averages					
Leaders	63%	70%	44%	45%	20%
Bread / Carbonated Soft Drinks	Dairy-Milk / Meat-Fresh	Produce / Salty Snacks			
Niche	33%	45%	15%	34%	5%
Dairy-Yogurt / Canned Fish	Pet Food				
High Interest	80%	69%	55%	16%	9%
Bottled Water / Candy	Cookies / Ethnic Foods				
Underdeveloped	41%	48%	20%	10%	2%
Baby Food and Beverages / Frozen Appetizers/Snacks	Body Soap and Cleansers / Oral Care	Shampoo/Conditioner / New Age Fruit Drinks	Brewed Teas / Peanut Butter, Jam/Jelly		
Average	51%	54%	27%	22%	6%
Beer / Sports/Energy Drinks / Boxed Dinners/Side Dishes / Canned Fruit / Canned Entrees/Meals	Canned Soup / Canned Vegetables / Cereal / Coffee / Crackers	Dairy-Cheese / Frozen Dinners and Meals / Household Cleaners / Juice-Shelf Stable / Laundry	Paper Products / Pasta / Sala Dressing-Shelf Stable		

Figure 4.4   Leader categories close more sales.

Studies across a set of stores can show how different positioning of leader categories in the store can dramatically influence sales. Figure 4.5 shows the position of soft drinks and resulting sales for four different stores. Stores that locate these products on the perimeter "racetrack" of the store, whether front or back (as shown in the right-hand side of the figure), achieve significantly higher share of baskets with soft drinks in them, as compared to stores with this category principally located on center-of-store aisles (as shown in the left side). The better placement in the first store led to nearly a third of shoppers picking up soft drinks, as opposed to just 13 percent in the last store. Even attractive "leader" items such as soft drinks will not necessarily lure shoppers into the center aisles, but if they are placed in the path of shoppers, they will lead to sales. This indicates the tremendous opportunities retailers and manufacturers have for increasing sales by better placement of products in the store.

Most categories, however, would not have such a wide swing as carbonated soft drinks, since purchases per category, on a basket share basis, tend to be relatively constant across stores. Carbonated soft drinks, on the other hand, are unusually sensitive to regions, the weather, and so on. For instance, you can expect to sell more soft drinks on a per capita basis in July and August in the Carolinas than in the Dakotas in January and February.

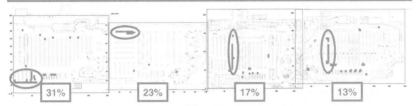

Figure 4.5 Shares of baskets with carbonated soft drinks across four stores

Breaking the Rules

There are no rules in active retailing that somebody isn't breaking very successfully, somewhere. They might be doing so consciously, deliberately, and with a clear understanding of the principles we have discussed—or not. While many passive retailers do well, active retailers who understand what they are doing based on measurable data will spot opportunities that would not otherwise be apparent.

Some examples are as follows:

- Costco CE Jim Senegal happily breaks the rules of active retailing—but he does so based on a clear understanding of what they are. He has, for example, been quoted as saying that he often gets challenged about two main issues in the store. The first is a lack of a directory so customers can find what they want. But, he says, maybe I don't want them to find things straight away. And the second is the lack of an express checkout for those buying only a few items. But why should he reward his poorest customers, he argues?

- Trader Joe's carries 100 percent private-label merchandise. Although the role of private label is increasing across the retail world, 100 percent private-label represents a niche in itself.

Playing the Niche

The niche group of products offers another prime hunting ground for potential sales improvements. These are products that are very good at closing the sale, but poor at stopping the traffic. Notice, though, that they reach the lowest percentage of traffic in the store. On the other hand, high-interest products often are placed in front of more traffic than any other category in the store, *including the leaders*! Why is this, when they are doing such a poor job of closing the sale? Like a lot of "salesmen," they talk a good game, but just don't get the job done. But retailers are fooled by the high interest in these products and fail to see that with the highest level of exposure and reach, they don't deliver sales to match. But the niche products can deliver respectable sales with minimal exposure. The key is to give them visibility from high-traffic areas, but not necessarily locate them within these areas.

What is the potential of niche products? We analyzed this question for a single superstore and found that the store was potentially leaving $2 million on the table because of its strategy for a single category of niche products. We compared the sales in the niche categories (baby food) to an opportunity index (market demand index) based on actual total store traffic, neighborhood demographics, and sales at other stores across the country. For baby food, this store was selling nearly $2 million less per year than could be expected. Simply exposing that category to more in-store traffic—moving it to a higher traffic area—could deliver $2 million of additional sales. (Notice that in this supercenter, baby food falls into the niche group, illustrating how a category's performance varies depending on specific store conditions. Across a national sampling of supermarkets, the average performance of baby food puts it in the under-developed group—poor stopping *and* poor closing.)

General guidelines for each of these categories are shown in Table 4.1. By more carefully managing each of these groups, retailers can put products in front of shoppers that they will stop and buy. And that will increase overall sales.

Table 4.1 Category Guidelines for Placing Products

Leaders	Leader categories should be put in very high-traffic locations and be given priority for secondary placement (end caps, placement on perimeter, and so on).
Niche	Niche categories require increased awareness. It is key to have visibility from high-traffic areas, but not necessarily placement in those areas.

High Interest	Conversion issues for high-interest categories are not related to layout/placement within the store. Investigate assortment, pricing, merchandising, and messaging opportunities for improvement.
Underdeveloped	Underdeveloped categories can be placed in lower traffic areas. The alternative is to increase awareness in these categories with unique offerings or positioning (as with new products).

Good Is the Enemy of the Great

Understanding these distinctions can help put the right products in the right place in the store. The right placement can help meet shoppers where they are and close a sale. It can allow the retailer to play a more active role in the process, without standing in the aisles and taking down items from the shelves. This understanding of shoppers and stores can help retailers make the creative leap of putting a line of nectar in the middle of a juice display. There are many other opportunities for rethinking approaches in the store that can boost sales.

This concept of distinctions overcomes the instinctive reaction to settle for what is merely "good." As Jim Collins wrote in *Good to Great: Why Some Companies Make the Leap…and Others Don't*, "the good is the enemy of the great."[4] In other words, if you settle for good performance of products and don't investigate what makes the leaders great, you won't outperform your competitors. In this case, we are considering retail strategy as well as the products themselves.

Endnotes

1. This might not matter, except that how categories are defined will alter significantly, not only the statistical performance measures, but also how they are conceived ever after. And the statistics that begin to be a baseline for our understanding tend to be set in concrete, based on what we include or don't include in any category. So, defining "dairy" to include chilled juices and refrigerated dough may make a lot of operational sense, including incentive pay for the dairy manager. But it can result in serious distortions of the "juice" market if juice is not identified separately in the dairy department. In other words, move one product to a different section, and the whole statistical picture changes.

2. "Product Packages Now Shout to Get Your Attention," *The New York Times*, August 10, 2007.

3. A quadrant analysis of this type has the usual advantage of dispersing the individual members (categories) so that their relative performance on two measures can be readily visualized. A disadvantage of the usual approach is always a central tendency, or clumping. We alleviate this problem by statistically identifying the central "clump" as average, and taking our cue from Joseph Juran, focus on those categories at the perimeter, the "vital few" most easily characterized, and most susceptible to specific creative management practices. In naming VitalQuadrants™, we follow the language of Paco Underhill and others, although our definitions differ to an extent.

4. Collins, Jim. *Good to Great: Why Some Companies Make the Leap...and Others Don't*, New York: Collins Business, 2001.

5

Brands, Retailers, and Shoppers: Why the Long Tail Is Wagging the Dog

"Whenever an individual or business decides that success has been attained, progress stops."

—Thomas J. Watson, Founder of IBM

There is a famous story about when Tesco started trials of its loyalty card, Clubcard, in the mid-90s. The retailer called on the services of Dunnhumby, a company specializing in data analysis. The results of these first trials were delivered to the Tesco board in November 1994—which led to a prolonged and awkward silence.

The board chewed over a 30-minute presentation about customer response rates, the impact on like-for-like sales, and a dazzling array of data collected from 14 stores. It was Sir Ian McLaurin, then Tesco chairman, who broke the silence with a now apocryphal remark. "What scares me," he said, "is that you know more about my customers after just three months than I do after 30 years."[1]

It might seem odd that a very successful retailer would know so little about its customers or what they do while shopping. Tesco and other retailers obviously are increasing their understanding of shoppers (although loyalty cards just tell what happens at the checkout, not in the store). In many ways, the massive problems in this industry are caused by everyone assuming that supermarket managements are the repositories of deep insight into the shopping process. By and large, they are not. There are a few exceptions—but they prove the rule.

There is a reason why retailers have historically paid so little attention to their shoppers—they are not rewarded for doing so. The economics of retailing are completely biased against it. We cannot explore the mind of the shopper without expanding our view to look at the broader—and shifting—relationship between retailers and the manufacturers of brands on their shelves. This complex and uneasy relationship helps explain much of what may appear to be counterintuitive about how retailers work. Understanding this relationship also highlights opportunities, which we discuss in this chapter, for brand owners and retailers to collaborate more effectively in selling products. Brand owners can help retailers redesign their stores to maximize sales and can also take advantage of powerful merchandising promotional planning programs to pitch the emotional messaging of each category more precisely.

Where the Money Is in Retail

If shoppers are ignored, it is because they contribute the least to retailers' bottom lines. This may be surprising, because on the surface the entire business model of a retailer seems to be to sell products to shoppers. But a closer look shows that this is only a front for the true business. The main sources of supermarket profits are, in order of importance:

1. **Trade and promotional allowances from the brand suppliers:**
   The number-one source of profits consists of rebates of one variety or another from those manufacturers who want to "warehouse" their merchandise in the retailer's self-service stores. The sometimes-maligned slotting fees are, in reality, a rational warehouse operator's recovery of storage costs from those who want to take the available space. It has been noted that supermarkets make their money by buying (from the supplier), not by selling (to the shopper).

2. **Float on cash:** Stores necessarily manage very large amounts of cash. In fact, one executive pointed out to the author the large amount of "abuse" the store receives from shoppers, but then pointed out that this is compensated for by the fact that they leave "their cash on the counter." This cash is hurried to the bank to begin immediately accruing interest, or *float*. Float will multiply until the necessities of business require the dispersal of cash to suppliers, employees, and others, days, if not weeks later. In any event, the store wants to begin *instantly* accruing interest on its portion of that $14 trillion annual turnover of the retail industry. A few seconds of that interest would suffice to maintain most households for decades. This is the second major source of profits.

3. **Real estate:** Every major chain maintains a large real estate department that finds real estate to develop for stores, often in developing communities. In a few years, that developed real estate will likely be worth multiples of the initial investment—not carried on the books as profit, because it will be unrealized until the sale of the property itself—often decades later after the underlying business has paid for it many times over.

4. **Margin on sales:** This fourth source is not to be sneezed at, largely consisting of *service* departments, operated on the retailers' own prime in-store real estate—the wide perimeter zones or other high-traffic areas. This would include things like the meat department, in-store deli, pharmacies, and so on. Another growing area of profit is contract outsourcing, where outside suppliers manage certain aspects of the operation (such as cafes/restaurants or flowers) and the retailers get a share of the margin from the contractor.

When these sources of profit, and the inherent nature of self-service, or passive retailing, are made clear, it is not surprising that retailers don't know a lot about the actual behavior of the shoppers in their stores. Why should they? The shoppers have been assigned responsibility for their own shopping, and aren't really complaining. But this is a dangerous and complacent position for retailers to be in because this passive methodology is increasingly being strained by the diminishing effectiveness of outside-the-store communication.

The reason the long tail is wagging the dog in retail is that brand owners are investing in promoting their many products in the long tail. As long as manufacturers are putting up the money, it makes sense for retailers to keep their large warehouses well stocked. But if shoppers are buying largely from the "big head" store, could retailers and manufacturers work more effectively in meeting this need?

The reason the long tail is wagging the dog in retail is that brand owners are investing in promoting their many products in the long tail.

Massive Amounts of Data

In addition to this economic imperative, there is another major factor driving the lack of interest in what is going on *inside* the store. That is the massive amount of information about what is coming *out of* the store, or the veritable flood of data spewing out of the scanners around the world. This scan data has spawned two major industries in their own right: compilers and resellers of the categorized data—Nielsen and IRI being the preeminent examples—and the advanced analytics relating this data to specific shoppers through the use of loyalty card programs, demonstrated by Dunnhumby and related businesses.

As positive as these derivative businesses are, neither speaks well of the retailers' own understanding of the shopping process. First, for decades, electronic barcode scanners contributed little more than an expedited method for ringing up the shoppers' purchases. Of course, sales data was more reliable for inventory control than the older warehouse velocity measures such as those provided by SAMI, which measured movements of goods based on warehouse withdrawals to the stores. But pricing and inventory control hardly bathe the retailer in glory for its use of shopper insights.

In fact, the salutary effect of Dunnhumby on Tesco only serves to highlight the deficiency of the retail giant's previous approach to the business. And now there is an ever-growing cadre of Dunnhumby-type firms who are surely accelerating business and profits for any number of retailers through advanced analytics of the scan data linked to the loyalty cards of individual, specific shoppers. So, just imagine the impact on profits of going even further and measuring what is going on in the actual *shopping process* in the store.

This is the stark reality that drives a good deal of retailing. It's not that retailers and suppliers don't seek to have a relationship with shoppers, but that their own mutual relationship tends to cause those to the shoppers to pale into insignificance, and, as a result, to remain somewhat distant by comparison. This is the reality of the self-service, warehouse-based view of the store. Sometimes my views may seem too critical, but there are certain absurdities in the industry that are driven by the economic structure. In the U.S. alone, fully one trillion dollars is paid by brand suppliers for the supermarkets to manage their supermarkets in a certain way.

To me, this is the emperor with no clothes. This is why supermarket managers measure inputs and outputs of the store but are largely blind to the process occurring in the store. And this blindness is shared by their brand suppliers. It is essentially the $1 trillion that the brands are paying retailers that justifies their leaving the $80 million per store on the table through not understanding and serving shoppers better. Of course, we have no illusions that there really is, in aggregate, an extra $80 million per store available to every store. But exceptions such as Stew Leonard's, with its $100 million stores, shows that much more is possible.

Shifting Relationships

The relationship between manufacturers and retailers is already shifting with the rise of private-label brands and the increasing marketing sophistication of retailers. In an October 2008 article in *Advertising Age*, Jack Neff reports how retailers are hiring talent away from consumer goods companies, measuring shoppers, and building their own brands—"raising big questions about the balance of power in the industry."[2] Retailers are increasingly focused on building their own brands rather than turning over their stores to manufacturers. This is neither good nor news to the brands. However, the role of brands is often not well understood or represented at retail. It helps to consider that when shoppers purchase branded items, they are acquiring three distinct values:

- **Intrinsic value:** A carbonated beverage will quench your thirst and meet your physiologic need for water.

- **Added value:** Packaging the beverage and delivering it to you in a convenient, and possibly chilled, form adds value to the intrinsic value of the water.

- **Creative value:** This third value is in the mind of the shopper and is the essence of brand value.

Because this third, creative value sometimes seems to be a gossamer wisp, it tends to be misunderstood and abused. It obviously has considerable commercial value, because all profits derive from the difference between costs and prices. The cost of intrinsic value is properly regulated by competition for basic, commodity resources. The cost of added value depends on manufacturing and distribution efficiency, including such things as cleverness of design. So what is the cost of creative value? Unit cost is zero, because once created, the more it is sold.

Once created, creative value is a bountiful source of profits. This is its strength and its vulnerability. The vulnerability is because those who do not own the brand are probably unwilling, at some level, to pay for it. This is the reason brands spend so much time and effort trying to convince the market that their value is really intrinsic or added. There is nothing wrong with a better mousetrap, and part of the value of the brand is the assurance that the brand will provide the "better" product.

But whether designer jeans or bananas, there is that something about the brand that makes a customer feel very good about spending a few pennies—or more than a few dollars—for it. In fact, that additional creative value is an important part of accelerating the upward growth of society. Think of that creative value as aspirational, something in the soul that longs for improvement and betterment.

In times of economic distress, there is always a call for a retreat to only intrinsic and added value. Retailers' first ventures in competing with their brand suppliers historically involved offering intrinsic plus added value private-label products only. The cutting edge today in retailing, however, is heavily dependent on building strong own-label brands, far removed from the old white label generics, as can be seen in retailers such as Trader Joe's. This is shifting the balance of power in retailing and placing more emphasis on understanding how shoppers interact with brands in the store.

While retailers have learned how to create brands (creative value), they have long assaulted the concept of brands by insisting on cutting prices to promote them. This strategy suggests to customers that brands were overpriced at their regular retail prices. Although the relationship between the manufacturer and retailer is often seen as a great struggle over the value created from shopping, this does not have to be the case. In fact, as we consider next, both retailers and brand owners can often do better if they work together to serve the shopper better.

A Refreshing Change: Working Together to Sweeten Sales

Assuming that both retailers and manufacturers want to sell products to consumers, if they understand shoppers better, they can work together more effectively to use in-store marketing in more sophisticated ways. ID Magasin, for example, worked with chewing gum manufacturer Dandy, a business unit of confectionery giant Cadbury-Schweppes, to increase category sales by as much as 40 percent by introducing "refreshment cues" in the pre-checkout area of Swiss retailer Pilatus Markt.

In-store research in 2001 examined how shoppers interacted with chewing gum displays at the checkouts. The company filmed, interviewed, and counted thousands of shoppers at three checkouts, each of which was merchandised differently to enable comparison of different concepts. Representative customers were also fitted with a point-of-focus/eye mark recorder to identify the visual cues used in purchasing decisions. Researchers discovered that customers had stopped actively shopping by the time they reached the checkout. Because the customers were no longer shopping—just visiting—the products didn't have a chance of stopping, holding, and selling.

The researchers realized they needed a trigger to reignite the shopping mode at the checkout. And, because "freshening" is the overwhelming motive for purchasing chewing gum, researchers recommended that refreshment cues be introduced in the approach to the checkout area. The company then employed a group of experts to establish the visual elements that signal refreshment. The group recommended imagery that strongly communicated refreshment and which shoppers could instantly decode and associate with chewing gum. Dandy next commissioned in-store marketing material based on these signals for use in the key pre-checkout area. There were four graphic directions, each of which could be adapted for individual retail customers to promote the entire chewing gum category.

The next stage of the project was to confirm that refreshment and breath-freshening cues in the pre-checkout area do increase sales in the chewing gum category, and by how much. Dandy undertook research in two stores in Denmark, Kvickly supermarket and OBS hypermarket. Overall, nearly 20,000 customers were filmed at four checkouts in each outlet. Two checkouts per outlet had the trial setup and two provided experimental control. Dandy found that the new point-of-purchase material did indeed stimulate consumers to revert to shopping mode and attracted more of them to that checkout area. The new strategy increased the sales of all the categories represented in the display by an amazing 40 percent and Dandy's sales by up to 44 percent.

This is a major boost in sales just by retailers and manufacturers working together to understand shopper behavior. The retailer had to rethink its checkouts. The manufacturer had to rethink its in-store marketing. This is a different relationship than a passive retailer receiving stocking fees from a brand owner to gain shelf space. This is creating a more compelling sales opportunity for shoppers, reflecting an understanding of the three moments of truth for the shopper. If visitors are not converted to shoppers and shoppers are not converted into buyers, there is no sale. Working together, the retailer and manufacturer increased sales, which benefits both of them.

If we assume that both retailers and manufacturers want to sell products to consumers, if they understand shoppers better, they can work together more effectively to use in-store marketing in more sophisticated ways.

Beyond Category Management

As this example illustrates, collaboration between retailers and manufacturers can help both. This partnership between manufacturers and retailers moves beyond traditional category management to active cooperation in management of parts of the store, or even total store management.

To understand this evolution, we need to consider the evolution of the concept of category management over the last decade or so, as retailers and their brand partners began to realize they needed to take a more shopper-centric approach. Category management began in the early 1990s when Brian Harris of The Partnering Group set out a number of "best practices" for collaboration between suppliers and retailers. Basic category management, still in widespread use, involves retailers and suppliers using sales data to answer questions such as: How should the products on the shelf be segmented? What should the layout be? How can SKUs be optimized? How many items should be on the shelf? Which ones? More brands or fewer brands? What about different pack sizes?

The next level, category reinvention, has come to the forefront over the last few years. This is far more extensive, going beyond segmentation, assortment, and pricing decisions to include such elements as themes, fixtures, signage, size, layout, location, paths, adjacencies, flow, assortment, and planograms. This approach is becoming more prevalent because it is more engaging and encourages higher levels of conversion by offering a more emotional experience. A meat department, for example, might be creatively reinvented to look like a butcher shop. The coffee aisle might be redesigned to give a coffeehouse experience.

A New Era of Active Retailing: Total Store Management

Category management, aisle management, and even store management are blunt instruments. They lump products and categories together. Item management, on the other hand, is a scalpel, targeting the small number of items in the store that are major levers for sales. The typical approach to category management is for every category to have its place in the store. But if the individual products were instead totally randomized through the store, the shopper would be more exposed to more categories. Taking this approach to this extreme might lead to chaos, but secondary placements in the store do move retail in this direction by putting items in unexpected places, and managing individual items that drive store sales. The long tail of the store may be organized by categories, but the big head should be placed where shoppers can find it.

A third and higher level of category and aisle management is emerging, which is a natural progression from category management and the drive to create a real partnership between active brand owners and active retailers. Total store management takes a much broader perspective, with manufacturers working with retailers to design their total store layouts. This goes to the specifics for all the major categories, both in organization and arrangement in the main store, as well as in the promotional store. This progression from category management to aisle management and on to total store management can be seen as part of the accelerating movement from passive to active retailing that is now underway.

There are several reasons why this approach is attractive, particularly to larger brand owners. First, they often have products all over the store. Coca-Cola, for example, has products in the water section, in juices, in teas, and so on. Anything the brand owner can do to maximize the performance of the total store is going to improve its business. Second, when companies have a very large category—confectionery, say—overseeing the store in a holistic way means they can exploit their positions not just in the primary display areas, but also in the secondary, promotional display areas such as end caps and the checkout, where an average 30 percent of purchases are made. Instead of fighting for space in the center aisles where shoppers are reluctant to come, manufacturers can take their brands out to the shoppers more effectively by looking at the total store.

A sophisticated large European confectionery manufacturer, for example, worked with a major retail partner to determine the ideal layout for stores, addressing the following questions:

- **Identifying leaders:** What are the steering categories in the retailer's stores, which genuinely move traffic? Remember, there are typically a small group of categories that do move traffic, the leaders—the rest are just along for the ride.

- **Arrangement:** In which order should different categories within a given arrangement ideally be placed?

- **Interaction:** In what way is the usage of different categories influenced by the location of other categories?

- **Order:** What is the optimal order of planned categories, impulse categories, and the categories "in between" (if they exist)?

All these questions are essentially *behavioral* questions. That is, if we can understand exactly how all the shoppers *behave* in the present store, this will serve as the foundation guide to how it might be altered to enhance that behavior to the mutual benefit of shoppers, the retailer, and their brand suppliers. To study shopper behavior, researchers began by analyzing how shoppers move through the store. In this case, data was collected by "shadowing" shoppers, re-creating their trip with various behavioral annotations on a web tablet, as illustrated in Figure 5.1. The paths of individual shoppers were charted, as shown in the right side of the figure, and then paths of many shoppers were amalgamated. The methodology used here, *Personal* PathTracker®, is one of many methods for creating this data, including radio-frequency idenification (RFID) tracking, video tracking, or shopper vision tracking

Figure 5.2 shows the trip progression of these many shoppers in a stylized form. The numbers indicate how far along in the average shopping trip the shopper is, beginning at the lower left (0.7 = 7% of the trip) to 1.8 and 2.8 to the right, and so on through the store to the 9.2 at the end of the store. The numbers are across many shoppers so the reason it doesn't go from 0 to 10 is that no matter how many people are heading one direction, there is always someone going the other direction. If nearly everyone ends their shopping trip at the checkout, there will be someone who begins there and moves in the opposite direction, both in terms of traffic flow, on the right, and time point (progression) in the trip. The arrows in the right side of Figure 5.2 represent the dominance of traffic, not volume of shoppers. (A small arrow, for example, means that the number of people flowing both ways is about even. A larger arrow means that traffic is predominantly in that direction.) The researchers used the metrics summarized in Table 5.1 to understand shopping behavior in the store.

Figure 5.1 Shadowing shoppers, researchers follow shoppers and take notes on a web tablet.

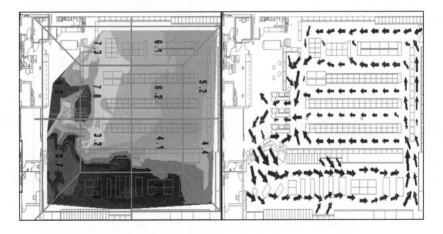

Figure 5.2 The progression of shoppers, showing patterns of movement

Table 5.1 Metrics for Shopper Behavior

For Every Category in Store	For Every Shopper
Reach (visit %)	Duration of shopping trip (seconds)
Stopping (shop % divided by visit %)	Proportion of store visited (%)
Closing (purchase % divided by shop %)	Proportion of categories visited (%)
Holding: of buyers (buy time— seconds)	
Holding: of buyers and nonbuyers (dwell time—seconds)	
Trip progression (% of trip completed at the point in the trip)	
Walking speed (feet per second)	

The complete flow and adjacency analysis produced six key insights, as follows:

1. **Understanding store and aisle traffic flow, hot spots and cold spots, and target shopper segments:** Researchers gained insight into the dynamics of movement of individual shoppers, as well as the overall flow of the crowd. This allowed identification of points of congestion and fixture location issues that might restrict traffic flow to all parts of the store. The goal was to open up and encourage traffic in an orderly way, to maximize the opportunity to offer the shopper the right merchandise at the most receptive point in their shopping trip.

2. **Identifying "leader" categories—high performers for stopping and buying power:** These "leaders" may be identified in the Vital Quadrant™ analysis discussed in Chapter 4, "Active Retailing: Putting Products into the Path of Shoppers." There we saw that there is not an iron-clad identity of these across all stores, but certain categories do appear again and again on the leader list. We also identified a series of categories through statistical clustering of shoppers by their trip behavior, which

are common to the largest groups of shoppers, whether for quick, fill-in, or stock-up trips. Even though the metrics and analytical approach are not identical, there is significant overlap between the groups.

Other independent groups, working with RFID trip data, using intelligent agent modeling, found a similar group of categories whose impact on the shopping trip accounted for the total store traffic, in terms of density and flow. This type of convergence from multiple analytical approaches gives us added confidence, not only in the role of the leader categories, but also that the great majority of categories in the store *do not* drive shopping behavior and that purchases occur largely incidentally to those driven by the leaders.

3. **Determining the ideal placement of "leader" categories to maximize performance and improve flow throughout the store:** Categories with high stopping power (visitor to shopper conversion) are given priority early in the shopper's trip (progression). This gets the shopper started off on the right foot, by beginning to fill the basket early. This also means that they're willing to spend more time on these purchases, making more of them, because they will tend to shop faster and faster, or spend less and less time, the longer they are in the store. It is also helpful to consider category buy time, trip type, and level of planned or impulse purchasing of the category.

4. **Identifying leader category "affinities":** Affinity means that when one product is purchased, then another is often purchased as well. This analysis helps determine the placement of these affinity categories to maximize their performance and improve flow throughout the store. Because we have data on trip progression, we can then place these affinity categories in the right order in the path of the shopper.

5. **Placing remaining categories using similar analysis procedures:** Once the leaders are positioned, the remaining categories can be placed based on margins and relevance to the other categories, as well as the guidelines offered for niche, high interest, average, and underdeveloped categories.

6. **Identifying ideal placement, contents, and messaging for promotional (secondary) displays:** This is done through visual audits of stores—what's seen and what's not seen—as well as a detailed accounting of the exposure to shoppers of various end caps in stores.

The results for this specific store were impressive, with post-redesign surveys showing that shoppers were very satisfied with the results and were likely to recommend the store to others. Specific sales lift improvements cannot be disclosed, due to proprietary concerns, but management consistently reports sales increases from a few percentage points to double digits after active retailing redesigns.

Pitching a Category's Emotional Tone More Precisely

One of the biggest questions retailers and brand owners have to answer is how to promote individual categories in the store. What should the emotional tone of each one be? Siemon Scammell-Katz introduced a set of powerful tools for merchandise promotional planning to address the type of promotions appropriate for various categories.

The foundation of the methodology was the evaluation of in-store shopping metrics from a large number of shoppers in a single UK supermarket linked to data from the same shoppers, as tracked over years in the TNS World Panel. Researchers found that two of the most significant variables in conversion rates are Buy Time (how long the purchase takes in minutes) and Purchase Frequency (on an annual basis). This analysis helped identify the emotional involvement of different categories. The categories are divided up based on these metrics and then restated in terms of the emotional mindset that shoppers are likely experiencing, given their investment of time in the purchase and its frequency, as illustrated in Figure 5.3.

Those emotional mindsets then provide guidance for appropriate communication strategies, to reach shoppers with the right type of messages, for the right emotional states associated with specified categories. For example, the categories that are high frequency but low involvement are most likely to be staples (in the lower-right quadrant). This, in turn, leads to a rational communication strategy appropriate to the category. For staples, for example, it should be about range reduction and ease of shopping. For "enjoyment" categories, it should be "theater," and for "involvement" products, the focus should be on providing information. Although this is a practical scheme for managing communication strategy in the store, it does not, of course, dictate the creative strategy. As noted earlier, a hot pink package might capture attention but may not make the sale, so there is plenty of room for creativity in communication.

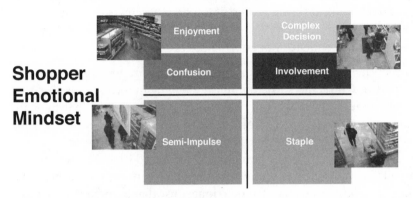

Figure 5.3 Connecting with the shopper's emotional mindset

The examples we have used for illustration are largely drawn from supermarkets and consumer-packaged-goods (CPG) or fast-moving-consumer-goods (FMCG) retailing. Our largest experience has been in this arena. But the most valuable asset here is not the massive normative database providing insight to CPG/FMCG, but rather the organized, scientific approach to retailing. We have applied this schema across a broad spectrum of retail trade around the world, including sectors such as autoparts, home electronics, phone stores, gift/card stores, clothing, jewelry, and so on. Moving from country to country (discussed in more detail in Chapter 8, "Multicultural Retailing") and across classes of trade changes the values of the metrics, but it does not change the organizational paradigm. Wherever we have gone in the world, we have found that most people are right-handed (hence the inherent trend to navigate a store in the counterclockwise direction). In similar fashion, across wide swathes of human behavior, there is more that makes us alike than different.

Retailers Control Reach

One challenge in the traditional relationship between retailer and brand owner is that the retailer controls the first stage of the sale: reach. Retailers control the design and layout of the store, so brands usually need to work within this framework. The passive retailer views reach as visiting: It's the shopper's responsibility to visit a product if they want it. Passive retailers also want to keep shoppers in the store as long as possible, so if products are difficult to find, or inconveniently placed, they reckon they are doing their job well. This attitude, which is locked into so many retailers' minds, is unhelpful. Supermarkets, for example, usually put the milk at the far corner of the store because they believe it will make people go there. Well, they very possibly won't. Instead, they may stop at the convenience store or a competitor if it's easier.

This creates great problems for brands because brand suppliers have to work through retailers to accomplish *anything* in terms of reach. First, people tend to shop with the subconscious expectation that they are going to buy just so much "stuff." Once they have the right amount, they are going to leave the store as quickly as they can. They are not going to anguish over whether they have Brand A or Brand B. In fact, even if they usually buy a particular brand, and the retailer moves it elsewhere, the shopper might not realize it and no longer use that brand for some time, if at all. This is the real challenge for the brand owner: The retailer is relatively indifferent about what people buy as long as it is a reasonable amount and they do so with some frequency and efficiency. Brand owners try to address this careless attitude through promotional fees, but it is a crude instrument. Brands make the real difference in stopping power—once the shopper comes into the product's orbit, but the shopper first has to get close enough to see the brand. To address this challenge of reach, brand owners need to work with retailers to more effectively position the brand in the store.

Once the shopper comes into reach of the product, its "visual equity" from branding and packaging makes a huge difference, particularly among the crowded long tail products. Packaging is the number one communication vehicle at retail. It is the most viable method the brand has for communicating with shoppers. The shape and color of the package—visual equity—that consumers associate with the brand (such as Coca-Cola's color red) allow the consumer to quickly identify products among the clutter at the point of purchase, in the pantry, or on the tabletop.

The Urgent Need for Retailing Evolution

Retailers are harvesting massive cash from the brand manufacturers for representation in the promotional area. Meanwhile, brand manufacturers are spending further billions on researching how to manage the main store. The two parties are both distant from actual shopper behavior—to the financial detriment of both. These economics are the foundation of the supermarket's profits but are killing the brands, whereas the shoppers tolerate this modus operandi because so far there are not many options.

We reemphasize here that we are not advocating retail revolution but are excited about the continuing evolution and hope to contribute to it and perhaps accelerate it. What we want to eliminate is the thinking that says: "Shoppers are in the store, and it is just too difficult to conduct research there. And it is also much too difficult to master the promotional store. So we, as the brands, will continue to invest in aisle/shelf management. And we, as the retailers, will continue to develop our promotional store for ourselves." They should both be focusing more attention on the promotional store—the big head. That is where the money and the opportunities are.

We also suggest that the strategy of putting promotional pricing on the items on the end caps is seriously misguided. Instead of trying to train shoppers to think: "If I want to get a deal, I should just grab something right here," they should think: "If I want a deal, I know I'm going to go down that aisle to get it." Retailers and brand owners should understand that their pricing and promotional strategy is highly irrational.

Brand suppliers, meanwhile, need to know how to maximize and optimize their secondary display performances: where the displays should be, what kinds of products should be on them, the type of message to attract the shopper and convert them to buy, and so on. It is not that brands do not work in this second store but that, because it is far more complicated and difficult, the focus tends to be on the section of flat wall in the main store over which they have some influence or control, and which is much easier to study and understand.

Promotional spending of big brands distorts the shopping experience in ways that are not good for the shopper, the retailer, and, often, even the brand owner. If I were a retailer, I would fiercely manage the big head strictly for the benefit of the shopper, and insist that the promotional "crack cocaine" not override the behaviorially expressed wishes of my shoppers. If you don't know how to manage the big head part of the store strictly in the shoppers' interest, learn or retire. I would continue to allow the long tail to be a battleground for the brands—and profitable for them, too. But the rational ones of them will want to know what they are getting from their share of that trillion dollars of retail spending.

No problem. It is urgent that you know the value of every inch of real estate, every aisle location, every end-aisle display, every shipper, every lobby display, and all the in-store media. I'm talking about approximately monetizing every inch of the store.

Endnotes

1. www.thecrossbordergroup.com.

2. Jack Neff, "Brand Giants Weakened as Retailers Get Savvier," *Advertising Age*, October 6, 2008.

PART II

Going Deeper into the Shopper's Mind

6

The Quick-Trip Paradox:
An Interview with Unilever's Mike Twitty

As discussed in Chapter 1, "The Quick Trip: Eighty Percent of Shopper Time Is Wasted," the quick trip has become the most common unit of shopping, yet most retail stores are designed primarily for stock-up shoppers. We interviewed Mike Twitty, Shopper Insights Director of Unilever Americas in the U.S., who has conducted pioneering research on quick-trip shoppers. As he notes, although quick trips account for about two-thirds of shopping trips, shoppers buy many different types of products on these trips. This is the Quick-Trip Paradox. This means catering to the quick tripper is not as simple as defining a small set of "quick trip" products.

How do you define a quick trip?

Twitty: In Unilever's research, the term "Quick Trip" is a relative term that shoppers use to describe the amount of time, effort, and money they invest in a given trip to a retailer.[1] Shoppers spend an average of about $100 on Major Stock-Ups, about twice what they spend on Fill-in Trips (about $50), and four to five times what they spend on Quick Trips (about $20). Because Quick Trips are relative, they vary in size, depending on the retail outlet visited. A Quick Trip to a club store is substantially longer and has a higher spend (about $44) than a Quick Trip taken to a convenience store (about $15). One way to think about the terms "Quick Trip," "Fill-in Trip," and "Major Stock-up Trip" is that they represent three different sizes of trips: the small, medium, and large trips that most shoppers take to their retailers.

The Quick Trip is different in frequency and purpose. In our research, we found that shoppers took an average of about 10 trips per month that resulted in a food purchase. Six of these were Quick Trips, and only one was a Major Stock-up Trip. Fill-in and Major Stock-up Trips both focus on buying items for the longer term or for restocking the household or pantry. Quick Trips, in contrast, are focused on buying items that will be used shortly after purchase, usually the same day or the next.

If you spend enough time watching shoppers in most retail outlets, you will notice, among other things, that few of the shoppers actually shop the whole store. In addition, if you read the research that measures actual shopping behavior, rather than what shoppers *say* they do, you will see mountains of data showing that most consumer packaged goods (CPG)/food shopping trips are composed of a small number of items per basket. Considering these two observations, one obvious question is "why?" This simple question has driven a whole body of research aimed at understanding shopping trips, the shopping decisions that take place outside of the store, and how they affect the behavior that takes place within.

Why do shoppers make so many quick trips?

Twitty: The simple answer is: because they can. Because we have easy, affordable access to so many retail outlets, shoppers often choose to get what they want as they discover they want it. Instead of having to organize their lives around the availability of the retailer, they develop strategies to use the abundance of available retail options, "cherry picking" them to best serve their changing needs. Although shoppers use a variety of strategies, the important thing is this: Most shopping trips to buy CPG and food items are Quick Trips, and Quick-Trip shopping is a unique opportunity for manufacturers and retailers.

Quick Trips are a byproduct of our affluence and its effect on both U.S. households and our retail space. If we flash back in time, to some 78 years ago, the first supermarkets appeared on the U.S. landscape, and shoppers of King Cullen and Ralph's delighted in taking advantage of two key benefits they offered: self-service and one-stop shopping. At that time, there were many fewer retail outlets, and shoppers had fewer opportunities to buy. In those days, shopping trips were infrequent, and planning before each trip was more important because running to a nearby store whenever you needed something was just not an option. Over the years, however, more and more retailers offered the items found in grocery stores and more and more retail space was built. Simultaneously, food and CPG items were also beginning to take smaller percentages of our growing incomes.

Looking over the course of time since the first grocery stores were created, we can see that as our household affluence increased and our retail options multiplied, the value of one-stop shopping declined. Today, we believe that with the great supply of retail alternatives available, when household money supplies expand or are in great supply, there is less of a need for one-stop shopping. When household money supplies contract or are in short supply, the value of one-stop shopping increases.

Although it is true that one-stop shopping and stocking-up are more economical ways to shop because they decrease the number of trips we take, our comparative affluence and easy access to retail has reduced our reliance on this practice. It follows, then, that quick trips are a convenience that has been enabled by easy, affordable access to retailers.

Another appeal of Quick Trips is that they enable shoppers to spend less time and effort planning. Quick trips make our lives more convenient by allowing shoppers to avoid the time and effort of planning before a shopping trip and by minimizing the need to live our lives limited by making sure that we have access to the resources available from our homes. Instead, shoppers can go more places and do more things because they can replenish their resources practically wherever they travel and whenever they choose. Regular stock-up shopping still takes place, usually on a weekly basis, and is vitally important in most households, but shoppers find themselves taking frequent, smaller trips to supplement their Major Stock-up Trips. Although it's true that increasing costs of shopping trips can change this pattern of shopping, for now it appears that Quick Trips are still the way that the majority of CPG and food items are shopped for.

How do pre-store decisions affect the quick trip?

Twitty: Before they enter a store, buyers of food and packaged goods have a relatively clear idea of what they want, and this knowledge steers them to visit some parts of the store while avoiding others. Unilever research shows that about 70 percent of all category purchase decisions (the decision to buy a product category such as mayonnaise or shower gel) occur *before* shoppers get to the store. Recent research from OgilvyAction found a similarly high percentage of such decisions were made outside of the store.[2] Such pre-store decisions also play a great role in determining how much shoppers will spend on that trip. For manufacturers, understanding and influencing shopping behavior outside the store is at least as important as understanding and influencing what happens within. For retailers, some argue that leveraging shopping behavior outside the store is even more important, because it often determines whether the shopper will visit their store on a given trip.

As soon as a consumer decides to get something they need or want, they become a shopper, and shoppers have lots of decisions to make. Two of the more important decisions they will make are which store or stores they will choose to visit to get the items they seek and what type of trip they will make. In this context, the words "type of trip" are a kind of shorthand that describes the shopper's objectives for a given trip and the personal resources they choose to invest in that excursion.

What factors do consumers consider in deciding where and how to shop?

Twitty: For any given shopping trip we might choose to take, there are three primary considerations that shape the trip: 1) What do we need or want?; 2) How much money do we want to spend for what we need or want?; and 3) How much time and energy are we willing to devote to acquiring what we need or want?

Shoppers pit these considerations against their knowledge of the retail landscape to determine where their investment will take place. There are a host of other important considerations that follow these three, especially when focusing on shopping behavior within the store, but these three seem to be the most important considerations that determine the type of shopping trip they take and which store(s) will be visited.

How do consumers think about shopping trips?

Twitty: Using our "Trip Management" research method, Unilever has studied over 20 million trips and years of household tracking with the general population and key subgroups, such as Hispanics and baby boomers. We pioneered the method in 2004, which enabled shoppers themselves to classify the types of trips they took, based on trip definitions determined from prior ethnography. Shoppers also indicated where the trips were taken and what was purchased. In addition, shoppers provided the researchers with their register receipts to validate the shoppers' claimed behavior. This research was the first time CPG shopping trips across all major retail channels in the U.S. were measured attitudinally and validated with actual purchase behavior. The result was a powerful look across the major retail channels and retailers, as well as most CPG categories. It provided new insight into how people shop for CPG/food categories and how they use retailers to achieve their shopping goals.

One important distinction from other shopper studies is that the trip classification in this research was done by the shoppers themselves, rather than inferring or guessing at the shopper's motive based on the items purchased. The way it was done was very simple. After each shopping trip that included a food item, shoppers were asked to answer two basic questions about the trip:

1. How would you best describe this trip?

   - Major Stock-up Trip

   - Fill-in Trip

   - Quick Trip—to get a few items for a meal to be eaten within the next day or two

   - Quick Trip—to get a few items

2. What was the MAIN reason for the trip?

   - To re-stock the pantry or kitchen

   - A routine grocery shopping trip to buy items for today

   - A routine grocery shopping trip to buy items for the next day or two

   - To get an urgently needed item or two, quickly

   - To take advantage of a special offer

   - Just to get out, to look around, or have fun

   - To shop for a special occasion (for example, for guests, a party, or the holidays)

   - To get "ready-to-eat" items to eat/drink right away or before I return home

   - To purchase a nonfood item (but I eventually purchased a food item)

All household shopping trips that resulted in a food purchase were tracked over a two-week period, resulting in over 4,400 trips from about 900 households, across all major retail channels and most CPG/food categories. Since this first study, we have removed the limitation of looking only at trips that resulted in food purchases and now track households over the course of a year or more rather than just two weeks. Looking at all of these results has enabled insight into the basic patterns of CPG/food shopping.

What did you learn from this research?

Twitty: Quick Trips are the most common trip for consumer packaged goods or food shopping. Shoppers classify the majority of their trips to buy CPG or food items as Quick Trips. In Unilever's original research published in 2004, "Trip Management: The Next Big Thing," 62 percent of all trips were classified by shoppers as Quick Trips, as shown in Figure 6.1.

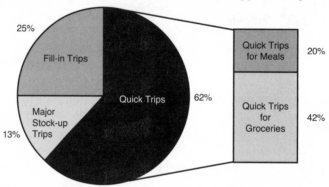

Quick Trips Are the Most Common Type of Trip

Figure 6.1   When shoppers define their shopping trips as either Quick Trips, Fill-in Trips, or Major Stock-up Trips, Quick Trips are the most common trip they report when buying groceries.

In recent Trip Management research where 11 million Nielsen-measured trips to all retail channels were monitored over the course of 2007, and all CPG trips were included, we found that 64 percent of the trips to purchase CPG categories were Quick Trips.

That such a high percentage of trips were Quick Trips was eye-opening, but what was absolutely shocking was that Quick Trips were the most common type of trip to *every* major retail channel—warehouse clubs and supercenters included! This finding has been confirmed every time the study has been replicated.

How could it be that even warehouse clubs and supercenters—whose design so strongly encourages stock-up shopping—receive more quick trips than stock-up or fill-in trips?

Twitty: The answer is that on most trips, shoppers are using these stores in ways that make the most sense for their busy lives and in ways that are possible simply because they have the financial resources to do so.

Figure 6.2 provides a great deal of information about the way shoppers use retail channels. You can easily see how shoppers use the different retail channels and the relationship between the size of the retailer's box and the types of trips that shoppers take there.

Types of Trips Taken to Each Retail Channel

	Warehouse Clubs %	Super-Centers %	Healthy Grocery %	Super-markets %	Specialty Stores %	Discount/ Mass Stores %	Dollar Stores %	Chain Drug %	Conv. Stores %
Major Stock-up Trips (%)	26	14	9	12	7	5	3	2	9
Fill-in Trips (%)	29	33	32	25	23	21	20	10	
Quick Trips (%)	45	52	59	63	71	74	77	88	91
% of All Grocery Trips That Go to Each Retail Channel	5%	10%	1%	66%	1%	4%	3%	4%	2%

Figure 6.2   Quick Trips were the most common type of trip for every retail channel, even warehouse clubs and supercenters.

Given that quick trips account for two-thirds of shopping trips, how can retailers and manufacturers cater to these shoppers?

Twitty: It would seem that all we have to do is understand what shoppers buy on Quick Trips and we would have the basis for serving them better. Unfortunately, this is where things begin to get difficult. Looking at the

2007 data (featuring Nielsen's Syndicated Category definitions and purchases from all outlets), we can see the troubling observation we call the "Quick-Trip Paradox."

What is the Quick-Trip Paradox?

Twitty: The paradox is that although most shopping trips are Quick Trips, these shoppers are not coming to the store for the same products each time. In fact, we found that the average CPG category is purchased on a Quick Trip just 38 percent of the time. Quick Trip shopping must be composed of a very broad and changing variety of CPG categories. In a single week, a household might make a Quick Trip for milk, chips, and beer on one day, whereas a day or two later they might take another Quick Trip seeking light bulbs and paper towels. The following week might see a Quick Trip for antiperspirant, shampoo, and mouthwash. There just isn't a concise set of related categories that would satisfy the range of shoppers' needs on Quick Trips.

There are a wide variety of products that draw Quick-Trip shoppers to the store. This is a substantial impediment for anyone hoping to capitalize on the Quick Trip by dedicating retail space to serve these trips efficiently.

> The Quick Trip Paradox: Although more than 60 percent of shopping trips are Quick Trips, the average consumer packaged good category is purchased on a Quick Trip only 38 percent of the time.

Given this paradox, how can retailers and manufacturers capitalize on the quick trip?

Twitty: Trying to identify the ideal assortment to satisfy the Quick Trip is maddening. There are no simple answers. Some categories are purchased more often on Quick Trips than the other trips. Out of roughly 120 categories, just 27 product categories are purchased mostly on Quick Trips. Table 6.1 is a ranking of categories that are more likely to be purchased on a Quick Trip. The categories that have the highest percentage of their purchases occurring on Quick Trips are at the top of the list. The table below excludes infrequently purchased categories, categories that are purchased on less than 1.5% of all trips.

Table 6.1   Top Categories That Are Purchased Most Often on Quick Trips, After Removing Slow-Moving Categories

Category	% Times Item Purchased on Quick Trip	% of Trips That Include the Category
Computer/Electronic Products	70.9	3.5
Tobacco and Accessories	70.4	4.7
Housewares/Appliances	63.6	2.0
Office/School Supplies	62.9	6.1
Light Bulbs/Telephone	60.6	2.1
Misc. General Merchandise	59.7	3.8
Cosmetics	58.3	1.9
Battery/Flashlight/Charge	56.8	2.9
Cough and Cold Remedies	56.1	3.1
Beer	54.2	3.1
Medications/Remedies	53.3	5.6
Grooming Aids	53.2	1.7
Candy	52.1	14.6
Vitamins	50.4	3.6
Pain Remedies	49.6	2.4
Skin Care Preparations	49.4	2.5
Wine	48.7	2.1
First Aid	48.4	2.4
Kitchen Gadgets	48.2	3.0
Pet Care	48.2	3.9
Gum	47.4	2.8

(continues)

Table 6.1 Top Categories That Are Purchased Most Often on Quick Trips, After Removing Slow-Moving Categories *(continued)*

Category	% Times Item Purchased on Quick Trip	% of Trips That Include the Category
Sanitary Protection	46.7	1.9
Hair Care	46.4	4.9
Oral Hygiene	42.5	5.3
Pet Food	42.1	9.5
Shaving Needs	42.1	1.8

Can you spot the link between these frequently purchased categories that are most likely to be purchased on Quick Trips? Is it clear what ties these items together? Can one understand what would be the best assortment and layout of a "Quick Trip retail space" by speculating on the underlying motivations of Quick-Trip shopping based on this list of categories? It's very difficult!

Could the shoppers' motives for making the trip offer insights into the best assortment to offer?

Twitty: What is it that shoppers are seeking when on Quick Trips? Shoppers told us that when they were on Quick Trips, they usually wanted to accomplish their shopping quickly, and as we have already said, they were seeking items to be used or consumed in the very near future, meaning that day or the next. Unfortunately, the range of products that can be needed somewhat urgently, for that day or the next, is staggering because literally every product category qualifies. So, it seems that neither the shoppers' known motives for taking Quick Trips nor the list of Quick-Trip categories provides the necessary insight to define a workable retail space tailored to serve the quick trip efficiently.

How can retailers best meet the needs of quick-trip shoppers?

Twitty: If we chose to assemble a collection of the most frequently purchased categories, we would probably have a much greater likelihood of attracting and satisfying those valuable shoppers who are in a hurry to get items they expect to use that day or the next. Stocking the most frequently purchased categories in a convenient way assures that you have the assortment for the broadest array of Quick-Trip shoppers. See Table 6.2 for the most frequently purchased categories across all outlets, as compiled by the Nielsen Company.

Table 6.2 Most Frequently Purchased Items (All Trips)

Category	% Times Item Purchased on Quick Trip	% of Trips That Include the Category
Bread and Baked Goods	33.4	23.4
Milk	34.0	21.0
Fresh Produce	28.0	18.4
Snacks	34.6	18.4
Carbonated Beverages	40.7	17.3
Paper Products	32.1	14.7
Candy	52.1	14.6
Juice/Drinks—Can, Bottle, and so on	29.6	14.5
Cheese	23.2	13.3
Packaged Meat	24.1	13.3
Condiments, Gravy, and Sauces	22.4	11.3
Cereal	26.4	11.1
Prepared Foods—Frozen	23.0	10.0
Pet Food	42.1	9.5
Vegetables—Canned	21.1	8.6
Cookies	33.8	8.4
Eggs—Fresh	26.2	8.2

(continues)

Table 6.2 Most Frequently Purchased Items (All Trips) *(continued)*

Category	% Times Item Purchased on Quick Trip	% of Trips That Include the Category
Prepared Food—Dry Mixes	21.7	7.8
Soup	22.3	7.7
Prepared Foods—Ready Serve	21.9	7.1
Vegetables—Frozen	20.6	6.8
Crackers	24.9	6.6
Dressing/Salad/Deli	24.8	6.5
Detergents	32.0	6.4
Butter and Margarine	19.2	6.2

Bread, milk, produce, snacks, soft drinks…these familiar, high-frequency categories may provide a better basis for building a reasonably efficient "Quick-Trip retail space." It would be a good idea to supplement this list with categories identified by a basket analysis against each of the most frequently purchased items. (A basket analysis identifies those items that are most often in the basket when a given item is purchased.) This analysis will identify the items most likely to be purchased, along with these high-frequency winners. Although it is focused on the most frequently purchased items rather than just those purchased on Quick Trips, organizing a retail space around these items seems to be a better basis for serving Quick-Trip shoppers—and all shoppers.

What are the implications for retailers and manufacturers?

Twitty: Retailers seeking to satisfy Quick-Trip shoppers should focus on how they manage their most frequently purchased categories. This is because satisfying shoppers on Quick Trips is not a simple matter of identifying those categories that are purchased most often on Quick Trips and making them conveniently available in a retail space. Quick Trips do not center around a limited number of items that are always purchased on Quick Trips. Quick Trips are composed of an impossibly broad array of items that are purchased on Quick Trips simply because they are needed for use or consumption on that day or the next. Such items range from soft drinks for immediate consumption all the way to items that are usually stocked-up on, such as light bulbs or batteries that, on this occasion, happen to be needed "right away" or for use in the near term.

Similarly, manufacturers should not be aiming to engineer products or "solutions" to be purchased on Quick Trips. Instead, they should focus on creating offerings that have high purchase frequency so that they have a greater likelihood of being purchased on any trip.

Endnotes

1. The terms "Quick Trip," "Major Stock-Up Trip," and "Fill-in Trip" have specific meanings in Unilever research so they are capitalized as proper names when used to refer to these definitions.

2. Ogilvy*Action*, Shopper Decisions Made in Store, 2008.

7

Integrating Online and Offline Retailing: *An Interview with Professors Peter Fader (The Wharton School) and Wendy Moe (University of Maryland)*

hile I have spent most of my career studying the click-click-click of shopping carts in physical retail stores, the click-click-click of online retailing has emerged as an important new window on shopper behavior. With new technologies moving into retail stores, and increasing integration of online and offline commerce, studying online retailing also provides insights into how shopping might evolve in the future. I had long been aware of Wharton Professor Peter Fader's shopper modeling studies in physical retail stores and have had a chance to collaborate with him in studying the in-store shopping process. In the late 1980s and early 1990s, he and other researchers used a growing avalanche of point-of-sale scanner data to analyze what people buy. Their models could help us understand, for example, why shoppers bought one brand of orange juice over another. While linking sales data to specific customers was a leap forward, it still offered limited insight into the behavior of shoppers in the store. Our work, as discussed in the book, initially helped fill that gap in the physical retail space, carefully observing and analyzing how shoppers shop.

But then came the Internet. In addition to his studies and modeling of physical retailing, Fader and his colleague Wendy Moe, associate professor of marketing at the University of Maryland, have conducted pathbreaking studies of online behavior. In studying their work on online shopping, I saw that the core principles bore a striking resemblance to what we see in physical stores. The point-by-point clickstreams of online shoppers are similar to the point-by-point visiting, shopping, and purchasing of in-store shoppers. Although I have focused more on "crowd" statistics in my work, looking for descriptive insights for all shoppers or major groups, Fader and Moe (along with other colleagues) have looked at patterns of individual shopper behavior as a means of assessing the drivers of individual behavior. The picture is richer from both perspectives than from either alone, and each confirms the other. In this interview, they share some of the insights from their research.

How did the Internet change the study of shopping behavior?

Fader: For my first ten years or so here at Wharton, I was looking strictly at point-of-sale scanner data, just analyzing what people buy and completely ignoring the context around it. Not that I wasn't interested in the context, but there was just no data. So, we had all these models trying to help us understand why people buy this brand of orange juice instead of that. The models worked great and people applied them to very different areas such as pharmaceuticals and financial services. Then everything changed with the dot.com revolution. As everyone was jumping into these uncharted waters, I initially wanted no part of it. I figured the process of someone standing at a shelf and deciding what juice to buy is going to be very different than someone sitting at the computer clicking through a bunch of different books or CDs—until I actually looked at the data, and it turned out that the patterns were remarkably similar. The same types of patterns were apparent in both purchasing *processes*. It was really fascinating. I never expected it.

Moe: I focused on online research from the beginning. My early research looked at online shopping behavior, how frequently people come to the store, how much they visit it, and what kind of search activities they use in comparison to other stores. That can give us an idea of how much they purchase. Then we can forecast their purchasing. We looked at patterns across visits and repeat visits to predict what they might buy in the future. I realized, however, that for some categories of products, consumers are not necessarily going to make repeat visits before they buy, so I focused on page-to-page behaviors within a single store visit. I looked at issues involving the focus of search behavior: Does one look at a specific brand or jump around across categories? Within a category? Is the consumer buying or just browsing? What do these patterns mean for purchase behavior?

E-commerce marketers have an abundance of data that most offline retailers don't have access to. They use this for better diagnostics and more accurate forecasting. They also can experiment with product layout and promotional messages. In the physical world, customer data have been focused mainly on when, what, and how much people buy. What researchers in physical stores haven't been able to measure as well are activities such as comparison-shopping and information gathering, which often have a strong influence on the final choice. Insights from online data might help offline retailers better understand shopping behavior.

> "I figured the process of someone standing at a shelf and deciding what juice to buy is going to be very different than someone sitting at the computer clicking through a bunch of different books or CDs—until I actually looked at the data, and it turned out that the patterns were remarkably similar." —Peter Fader

In what way are the online and offline patterns similar?

Fader: We found that people's tendencies to do something and decide whether or when to do it again—and how many more times to do it—were similar. The mathematical models describing the behavior could be applied in almost a "cookie cutter" way to a variety of products, from cans of baked beans on the shelf at the Safeway to books online at Amazon.com. I threw myself into e-commerce because there we could see not only what people buy, but also the process leading up to it. We began looking at the interplay between visits and purchases online. There were all these patterns that we could never see before that were consistent with what we had been seeing. Then we came across your PathTracker® studies in bricks-and-mortar stores, using RFID tags on shopping carts, and this allowed us to integrate these two areas of research, measuring shopper behavior with a variety of different tools (see the following box). We could take the rich context that we were able to see in the online world and marry it with our deep understanding of what happens in the grocery world. It allowed us to address questions such as: Which zone will you visit next? Are you just passing through or are you really shopping there? And if you're shopping there, what things, if any, are you going to buy?

The same shoppers move through a path and decision process in finding and buying, whether online or offline. Different research tools are used to track and compare the behaviors of these shoppers in these different environments, including the following:

- **Retail shopping:** Radio Frequency Identification (RFID) tags underneath shopping carts track consumers' in-store movements.

- **Eye tracking:** Researchers ask subjects to view print advertisements and capture their eye movements using infrared corneal reflection technology, or use the same technology in the store.

- **Web browsing clickstreams:** Consumers' web-browsing patterns are tracked by recording the sequence of web pages visited in a session.

- **Information acceleration:** Researchers immerse subjects in a multimedia environment to understand how they collect information and make decisions about a radically new product or service.[1]

How are paths in the supermarket similar to paths online?

Fader: Online and offline marketing both have path-type data associated with them, yet very few people consider the path aspects. They simply look at outcomes. Look at some of the e-commerce work on how people click from page to page and whether they are buying. I tended to think, like most people, that there's nothing else like it in the physical world. The Internet is brand new, right? But clicking through an online site is a lot like someone pushing a cart up and down the aisles. Turning left or right in the grocery store is a lot like clicking on this link or that link, even though the physical movements are quite different. The decision process, when you get down deep, appears to be pretty similar. A path is a path, whether it's online or offline, people or birds.

Can online retailers learn from offline shopper behavior?

Fader: Take a small example: Herb, your in-store research has found that shoppers tend to look to the left and move to the left, counterclockwise, as they move through the store. Where is the shopping cart located on just about every online site? On the right. You've got people who will experiment with absolutely everything in designing their website—different content, different colors, different everything. But the shopping cart is always on the right. They have no idea why. Should they test the cart on the left?

We should no longer be surprised when we see these online/offline analogies. We should expect them. But a lot of people don't buy it. They say, oh no, come on, looking at a screen is totally different than pushing a cart in a store. There's very little evidence to suggest that it's really different. On the other hand, offline retailers, who have spent all this time laying out the aisles and getting the merchandise at the right height, don't think they could learn something from online. But I believe they can. The ultimate irony is that bricks-and-mortar retailers are outsourcing their online business to online firms. They say: Make our website as efficient as possible and just tell us how much money we are making. These online companies are running thousands of different experiments every day. But they tend to be two completely different species of people, and they are not taking any of these learnings back to the offline store.

Some of the areas that we have studied that have implications for both online and offline retailing are crowding and herding, sequencing or licensing (buying "vice" products such as chocolate after "virtue products" such as vegetables, for example), shoppers speeding up as they move toward their goals, shopping momentum, the impact of variety, and hedonic shopping behavior.[2]

Tell me about what you've found out about crowd behavior?

Fader: Studies online and offline show similarities in crowding and herding. It boils down to this: If I'm in a store and I see a big crowd of people down an aisle, does it attract me or repel me? There are two schools of thought. One says that a crowd attracts people, the other that it repels.

But it's not that straightforward. People tend to go where there is a crowd—but they won't necessarily shop there. I see a crowd in a store, so I am going to push my cart down there to see what is going on; however, it might just be too crowded to engage with products on the shelf, so I'm going to move on. What we found is that it doesn't just depend on the individual but also on the type of behavior. We have some insights, but there is still a question about how these two forces counterbalance each other. This is an excellent example of why we need a statistical model.

It is also worth mentioning the connection here with GRPs (gross rating points) and their constituent components, reach and frequency. The question is: Do we want to get people staring at the shelf often, or do we want to get *a lot* of people to stare at the shelf? You might get a lot of reach but repel people at the same time because of the crowding.

What have you learned about licensing and sequencing—such as the purchase of vice items after virtue items?

Fader: There is a sequence in how people buy things. One important driver of this sequencing may be "licensing" behavior. If shoppers buy a virtue product—something good for them—then it gives them license to buy a vice product—something that they might enjoy but is probably not good for them. If they pick up broccoli or tofu in the produce section, they can buy the ice cream or chocolate cake or cigarettes. It has tremendous implications for the placement of products on the path through the retail store or online. This is one of the reasons why sequence matters. The chocolate cake at the beginning of the shopping trip might be viewed differently than at the end, when the shopper has accumulated some virtue products and now might be more willing to indulge in a vice.

We see this in the laboratory, but it has yet to be validated in the real world. We sit people down and show them a list of things and ask them to indicate which ones they would buy. But for certain people, you prime them by saying you've already bought a certain product (virtue or vice), and then see if they buy the vice product after the virtue. There is some variation across people in how attractive the vice products become after the virtue ones.

> "If shoppers buy a virtue product—something good for them—then it gives them license to buy a vice product."—Peter Fader

What have you found out about the pace of the shopping trip?

Fader: Research has shown that the closer you get to your goal, the more you speed toward it. This is called the "goal-gradient hypothesis." We see this in the context of loyalty programs, where people buy ten and get one free. A number of researchers have noticed that as you get closer to the goal, you speed up purchasing. This is consistent with what you've seen in the store, the concept of the "checkout magnet," where shoppers move more quickly as they get closer to the checkout. We could extend the goal gradient hypothesis beyond the checkout, to look at other goals that occur as you shop. They might be items on your shopping list, parts of the store that you go to on every visit—for example, to see if meat is on sale each week. This is difficult to study because, other than the checkout, shoppers have different goals. But we believe we will see evidence that this goal-gradient hypothesis applies to intermediate goals as well as the final checkout.

What have you learned about shopping momentum?

Fader: The idea here is that as more purchases are made, everything in the store becomes more attractive. Once shoppers pick up a number of items, it gives them the momentum to buy more. Once you have two or three items in your cart, you start really rolling and then pick up a lot of stuff. The more you buy, the more you buy. As your studies have shown, the most common number of items purchased in a grocery store is one. That means many shoppers never really get rolling. They may get that one item and, before they can be enticed to buying a second or third, they leave. If they do build momentum, they buy a lot more.

Just as with the other forces in play in the store, the impact of the forces at play such as shopping momentum will vary across individuals. That, again, is why we need a proper statistical model to measure the effect of these forces on individuals.

What have you learned about the role of variety in shopping?

Fader: There are some people who say that people like variety. If there's greater variety, then you're meeting people's needs in a better way and, therefore, the category as a whole becomes more attractive. On the other hand, if you have too many forms and flavors, as Barry Schwartz points out in *The Paradox of Choice*,[3] people are actually put off by too much choice.

We've only tested this so far in an indirect way—across categories, which is not the best way. We looked at categories that have high variety and those with low variety to see how attractiveness varies across them. What we see is that high variety is more attractive.

This doesn't necessarily refute your perspective or Barry Schwartz's that offering more limited selections can increase sales. We're looking across categories within stores, rather than the same category across stores, and there is tremendous opportunity for reverse causality here. It could be that if a category is more attractive, people really like it, and then retailers are going to want to stock more SKUs in it. That could explain why greater variety in a category is associated with greater attractiveness. There is a lot of testing that needs to be done.

What have you learned about efficiency? Is it better to allow shoppers to get quickly in and out of the store, or should retailers try to prolong the trip?

Fader: Traveling salespeople are famously well organized. They have to be: They are always on the move, visiting a certain number of clients every day, so they need to find the most efficient route possible. Our studies of the paths taken by 1,000 grocery shoppers at a store in the western U.S. have found that shoppers, unlike traveling salespeople, are often quite inefficient.[4] They might choose the right order in which to travel to find the products they want, but they take too long and go further off course than they need to. Another interesting finding is that inefficient shoppers tend to have more in their carts than those who shop more efficiently, so this inefficiency within reason is not necessarily a problem for retailers.

This research has major implications for both store owners and brand manufacturers. Retailers want their customers to have as efficient an experience as possible. On the other hand, they want the shopper to stay longer and interact with more products in the hope that it will drive more impulse purchases and incremental revenue and build the relationship that will make shoppers want to return. If, however, they prolong the shopping trip through confusing store design and bad signage, customers will get annoyed and not return. More time spent shopping could be a good thing if it is a sign of increased engagement but might be negative if it reflects confusion and aggravation.

In the online world, measurement has taken a radical turn from looking at how many unique visitors are attracted to a website to measuring time spent per session. Again, there is the divergence between efficiency and engagement: To what extent should retailers, whether online or offline, help shoppers finish shopping as quickly as possible or try to hold them for as long as possible?

Moe: I conducted a study on the impact of pop-up promotions on people's online surfing behavior.[5] People often complain that these advertisements are annoying. They don't like them. But actually they influence their behavior positively from the perspective of the retailer. People who are served pop-ups at the right moment actually stay on the website longer and shop and search a little bit more. If the pop-up itself has good content that matches their needs, visitors are encouraged to stay, search and buy. If the pop-up is on a gateway page—a home page or category page—that visitors use to get to the products they want to see, a pop-up is stopping them from getting to their ultimate destination. These are received poorly.

> *"People often complain that these [pop-up]advertisements are annoying. They don't like them. But actually they influence their behavior positively from the perspective of the retailer." —Wendy Moe*

This raises the question of whether shoppers are in the store for utilitarian reasons alone, or if they are interested in an experience. What is the difference?

Fader: Shopping can be for a utilitarian purpose—something that has to be done—or it can be done for a hedonic purpose—for the sheer enjoyment of it. Online grocery shopping has not caught on in the U.S. to the same extent as the UK. This might be because larger U.S. bricks-and-mortar stores offer the hedonic experience that online shopping lacks. Many Americans live in large houses spaced farther apart than their European counterparts, which makes going to the store more of a social experience. Again, this is an area ripe for investigation in both the online and offline world. In the online world, you can watch the same individuals over a number of shopping trips and start to notice patterns. Offline, what is needed is to marry data from a series of PathTracker® studies over time with data from a shopper loyalty card to find out exactly who is doing the shopping. This would show how often they are shopping hedonically versus in a utilitarian fashion and whether there were patterns involved.

What have you learned so far about what shoppers are looking for when they go online?

Moe: My research has looked at the underlying objectives of online shoppers and the expression of these objectives in purchases. I identified four distinct types of visits associated with different online behaviors, as follows:

- **Directed-purchase visits** are where the shopper enters the store with a clearly defined purpose of walking out with a specific purchase.

- **Search/deliberation visits** are utilitarian visits where a future purchase is being considered, and the store visit is designed to gather relevant information before buying.

- **Hedonic browsing visits** are more about enjoyment, where shoppers browse without looking for anything specific but might make an impulse buy.

- **Knowledge-building visits** are also enjoyable but are more geared toward collecting information for possible future purchases.[6]

It is important for online retailers to understand this to target their marketing activities effectively to the right people. Shoppers come into bricks-and-mortar stores for some of the same reasons.

How do online retailers use these insights about shopper visits?

Moe: The next stage of research looks at differentiating between online shoppers not just according to what pages they are looking at, but by also actually examining the products they are interested in.[7] In other words, what are the characteristics of the products they are searching for and interested in? And what are their ideal products? Building a model based on data from this research enables the retailer to estimate the probability of purchasing. For example, if someone looks only at a series of black shoes, you can infer that she has a clear preference for this color shoe. Someone else might be looking only at shoes in a certain price range. The sequence of pages tells the researcher something about what a person's preferences are. This helps predict not only *whether* they will buy, but also *what*.

By understanding better what shoppers are looking for, retailers can, in theory, create a virtual smart salesperson to help. This assistant might be compared to the salesperson in a physical store who, through observation and experience, can help shoppers find products they prefer while carefully screening out items they feel the shopper is uninterested in buying. A model of purchase expression could help create a virtual assistant that could do the same thing.

This captures the whole point of what we've called "active retailing." Online is leading offline in this area. How does this come into the physical store?

Fader: This has obvious implications for online retailing, but as more interactive technology comes into offline retail stores, through cell phones, PDAs, or other devices, it could also be done in the bricks-and-mortar world. To offer this kind of assistance, you need to understand shopper behavior and how it relates to purchases.

How do some of the complex forces of shopping behavior play out? Why is there a need for better modeling?

Fader: As we've discussed, there are sometimes countervailing forces in shopping. Crowds attract shoppers but might make them less likely to actually shop. (This is similar to the attraction of the "long tail" discussed earlier, which attracts shoppers to the store because they know they can get anything they need—although they may only buy from the "big head.") The checkout serves as a magnet to draw shoppers to the end of their journey, the goal gradient, but at the same time, shopping momentum makes shoppers absorbed in the process of shopping the more they shop, spending more time in the store. Efficiency is another area of balance. On the one hand, you want the trip to be as efficient as possible, so the shopper finds what he or she needs and leaves. On the other hand, you want to create engagement, to make the shopper stay longer and interact to drive more impulse purchases and form some kind of relationship. You also want variety, but not too much.

These forces counterbalance each other, which is why we need a statistical model to understand behavior. There is no way we can just look at the observed data and figure this out. These effects vary across people, and their interactions also vary across people. We need a proper statistical model that lets each person have his own momentum effect and each person have his own checkout attraction and to see if we can pull him out from the data.

What topics are you studying now?

Fader: A big issue we are looking at is edge detection in the "stores within stores" in what you call a "compound store." Since the edges of these stores are not always formally delineated, we are defining the way shoppers see different parts of the store. Where are the invisible walls? For example, if people tend to circulate within one area, it could be a self-enclosed zone. Why is that? How do they move beyond the borders of that area? Is it tied to products, or is there a psychological reason? We can study this through eye tracking and through models drawn from disease mapping, which look for clusters of diseases. There is a lot of scattered literature about how we can do this kind of boundary definition or edge detection, and we're just now starting to apply that to the grocery store.

Moe: I'm trying to refine the model for a virtual salesperson, as we discussed, and also looking at the role of online reviews. There is a lot of research that shows reviews have a significant impact on sales. If you have more positive reviews, or even just a higher volume, you get more sales. But the process of posting is something that we don't understand very well, and lots of managers and marketers and some researchers have speculated that there are biases in those reviews. Posted reviews tend to present more extreme views, so they don't really reflect the true quality of the product. I'm trying to separate the effect of that bias from the effect of true product quality. The purpose of doing that is that some marketers have started to seed some of these chat rooms and product reviews with their own comments to try and get the ball rolling. So the question is: Do these fake marketing posts have the same effect as an organic consumer-posted review?

Endnotes

1. Hui, Sam K., Peter S. Fader, and Eric T. Bradlow (2009), "Path Data in Marketing: An Integrative Framework and Prospectus for Model-Building," *Marketing Science.*

2. Hui, Sam K., Eric T. Bradlow, and Peter S. Fader (2009), "Testing Behavioral Hypotheses Using an Integrated Model of Grocery Store Shopping Path and Purchase Behavior," *Journal of Consumer Research.*

3. Barry Schwartz, *The Paradox of Choice: Why More Is Less*, New York: Harper Perennial, 2005.

4. Hui, Sam K., Peter S. Fader, and Eric T. Bradlow (2009), "The Traveling Salesman Goes Shopping: The Systematic Deviations of Grocery Paths from TSPOptimality," *Marketing Science*. See also (2006) "The 'Traveling Salesman' Goes Shopping: The Efficiency of Purchasing Patterns in the Grocery Store," http://knowledge.wharton.upenn.edu/article.cfm?articleid=1608.

5. Moe, Wendy (2006), "A Field Experiment Assessing the Interruption Effect of Pop-Up Promotions," *Journal of Interactive Marketing*, 20 (1), 34-44.

6. Moe, Wendy W. (2003), "Buying, Searching, or Browsing: Differentiating between Online Shoppers Using In-Store Navigational Clickstream," *Journal of Consumer Psychology*, 13 (1 and 2), 29-40.

7. Moe, Wendy (2006), "An Empirical Two-Stage Choice Model with Decision Rules Applied to Internet Clickstream Data," *Journal of Marketing Research*, 43 (4), 680-692.

8

Multicultural Retailing: *An Interview with Emil Morales, Executive Vice President of TNS Multicultural*

In addition to new technology that is changing retail, shoppers themselves are changing, with shifting demographics and the rise of multicultural retailing. This century is seeing dramatic shifts of population, and retailers are only just beginning to wake up to the changes they need to make to capitalize on these changes. In this interview, Emil Morales, executive vice president of the TNS Multicultural practice and general manager of their Centers of Excellence, explores this changing landscape, with a particular emphasis on the Hispanic population in the U.S. as an example of the global challenges of multicultural retailing. As he points out, many of these shoppers are coming from traditions of shopping at very small local stores, where clerks take a very active approach. Retailers need to take an active approach to meeting this segment, particularly with the added barriers of language and culture. Similar changes are occurring whether the multicultural customer is a Middle Eastern Muslim who has transplanted to Europe, a Hispanic immigrant in the United States, or a rural Chinese moving to one of the great cities of China. Morales examines how retailers need to change their thinking, product offerings, and store designs to reach this growing market.

This book looks at how retailers need to move toward active retailing by anticipating and responding to shoppers' needs. What does active retailing mean in the context of multicultural marketing?

Morales: First and foremost, you must understand the cultural norms, values, and needs of these consumers. Moreover, it is essential to know their geographic concentration and key demographics to provide the right products and services via the proper channels. Most new arrivals from developing countries are moving from a "service" retailing experience in small shops to one of self-service, which can be very impersonal. The developing world is characterized by neighborhood shops, where proprietors are hands-on and active in a very personal way. Rather than being educated about products and services by their local grocer, they are now required to learn in a physical environment, as well as a language and cultural setting, which is unfamiliar and even intimidating. This certainly slows progress for the retailer, manufacturer, and consumer. This means immigrants from developing countries may expect more active approaches, enabled by both new technology, such as smart carts and old tried-and-true methods that respond to their needs.

What are some of the challenges facing the multicultural shopper that retailers need to be aware of?

Morales: For those of you who have experienced foreign travel to a non-English speaking country, there inevitably comes a time when you need to make a purchase. You might be purchasing a power converter in an electric supply store in Paris, searching for a contact lens case in Amsterdam, or buying food items for a picnic lunch in Santorini. Needless to say, the experience creates feelings of both excitement and anxiety. In our daily lives, we rarely think about the shopping process. However, in a foreign country, the process takes on new meaning, as there are a number of steps to be considered. First, there is the language barrier. Even if you know what to call the item, you certainly will not pronounce it like a native, and you also need to express your search with more than a single word. Second, you need to figure out where to find the item, as you have likely discovered that where items are sold conforms to the norms of each country. Of course, figuring this out requires still more linguistic challenges. Once you know where it is sold, if you are lucky, you can simply walk there. If not, you need to deal with the logistics of travel to your destination. And then finally, you have to work through the actual cost in the local currency, especially if you cannot see the numerals on a display at the point of sale.

I count myself fortunate in having had such experiences, but it is also invaluable in helping to place myself in the shoes of the multicultural shopper. Although my struggles were temporary and also provided a sense of adventure and discovery, for those who have to maneuver the "stranger in a strange land" scenario every day with far more limited language and coping skills, it can be an exhausting and stressful experience. In fact, one only has to look at the number of American tourists who flock to a Starbucks in overseas locations to understand the importance of familiarity with the shopping process, as well as a product or brand. There is certainly an expectation that they will have what I want, they will understand me, and I will be in the company of like-minded individuals with whom I have something in common. It should come as no surprise that in the U.S., multicultural segments will behave the same way.

What is the significance of the Hispanic segment in U.S. markets?

Morales: Without question, one of the transformative events of the last several decades has been the explosive growth of the U.S. Hispanic population. Not only due to the sheer numbers, but most important, because it has caused an intense examination within the U.S. of our future national identity. Although Hispanics are often highlighted, the rapid growth of the U.S. Asian population and the emergence of a strong African-American demographic, as was evidenced in the recent presidential election, have a huge impact on U.S. society. The demographic shifts taking place are powerful and inexorable. By 2050, approximately 225 million people in the U.S. will be part of a multicultural segment. We're talking about almost a quarter of a billion people. It's a number that many marketers and retailers have yet to grasp. In fact, if you could convince these 225 million people to give you a dollar a day for a year, your total would be over $82 billion. Surely, a number like that will get retailers' attention. As shown in Table 8.1, according to the 2008 U.S. census, there are currently more than 46 million Hispanics in the U.S., about 15 percent of the population. The population is growing very rapidly. By 2050, Hispanics are expected to account for 30 percent of the U.S. population.

Table 8.1   Characteristics of the U.S. Hispanic Population

Figures	Facts
27.6	Average age versus 36.6 for total U.S. population.
46.7 million	Hispanics in the U.S. = 15.1% of U.S. population.
184%	Rate of growth: U.S. Hispanics estimated to hit 132.8M by 2050.
1.8%	Rate of growth: U.S. non-Hispanic white population to hit 199.8M by 2050.
30%	Overall Hispanic share of U.S. population by 2050.
40%	Current share of U.S. Hispanics who are foreign born.

Source: U.S. Census 2008

What makes this segment attractive to retailers and manufacturers?

Morales: By any measure, the U.S. Hispanic segment would qualify for serious investigation or investment. The Selig Center for Economic Growth in Georgia estimates that U.S. Hispanic buying power will reach $1.2 trillion by 2011. This figure exceeds by far the Gross Domestic Product of Mexico. McKinsey & Company, in their top trends published in 2006, stated that by 2015, the U.S. Hispanic population will have spending power equivalent to 60 percent of all Chinese consumers. These are large numbers and have already drawn the attention of retailers and manufacturers from across the globe, in particular those from Spanish-speaking countries, looking to leverage their brand equities in the U.S. It has also drawn interest in the investment community from companies such as Goldman Sachs, which has set aside $50 million to fund companies focused on marketing to fast-growing multicultural segments.

How can manufacturers and retailers seize this opportunity?

Morales: Serving the needs of U.S. Hispanics is not a simple task. Although all consumers have certain unique features of which retailers need to take note, U.S. Hispanics present their own set of challenges. For example, our research shows that close to two-thirds of U.S. Hispanics are either Spanish-dominant or Spanish-preferred. This translates into varying degrees of comfort not only with the written and spoken word, but also with entering environments where they may feel ill at ease. As we discussed, understanding cultural norms and creating welcoming environments are central to attracting and retaining these consumers. Their cultural norms dictate what they seek not only in terms of products, but also from retail environments. Figure 8.1 shows data from the most recent TNS Shopper 360 syndicated report. As you can see, U.S. Hispanics tend to shop many channels versus their non-Hispanic counterparts.

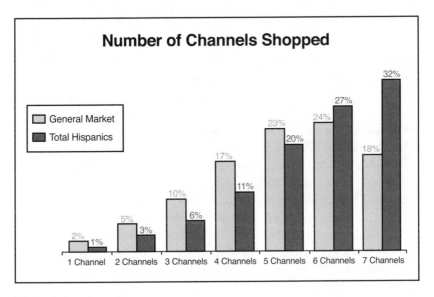

Figure 8.1   Channel use

Why do Hispanic customers shop so many channels?

Morales: This is due in part to the exploratory nature of their shopping behavior. You need to keep in mind that as many as 60 percent of U.S. Hispanics are foreign born and, therefore, are unfamiliar with the concept of so many channels. Approximately 65 percent of U.S. Hispanics come from Mexico and from many rural areas. Essentially, their exposure to channels was quite limited. As a result, they are often eager to learn what channels are available to them in the U.S. and what benefit each one offers.

Shoppers with limited exposure to U.S. culture are most likely to settle in communities where their language is still spoken and where many of the elements of their culture remain familiar to them. They might frequent local bodegas, or in the case of Mexicans, tienditas—small neighborhood stores. As their needs for more sophisticated products and services emerge, they will likely travel with a trusted friend or family member to a larger outlet—a supermercado (supermarket). There will likely still be people there who speak Spanish, the store will have the right cuts of meats and familiar brands—but there will be more of them. The environment will still be comfortable, however. Once they begin this process, it's not long before they move on to supercenters, club stores, and mass merchandise outlets, malls, and beyond. This is all a part of their enculturation into shopping in the U.S. However, getting them to visit and getting them to buy and remain loyal to the channel is not the same thing.

Trust is critical. The top reason given for store selection by U.S. Hispanic customers in the TNS Hispanic Shopper 360 study was "It is a store I can trust." In contrast, in the general market, the top reason cited was "could get to this store quickly." Clearly, the issue of trust is still central for Hispanic consumers. It's not too hard to think about why this might be the case. We all want to feel welcome and comfortable in our environment. We also want to know that if something goes wrong, we will be understood and treated with fairness. What these data seem to imply is that there is still room to improve in communicating a sense of trust to these Hispanic consumers. After all, we know that smaller bodegas and tienditas tend to charge higher prices and have less selection than larger-format stores, yet Hispanics still shop there. We know that the feeling of trust and comfort is important because they are willing to pay more for that comfort along with the convenience.

Given the popularity of tienditas and other small stores, do U.S. Hispanic shoppers have any interest in larger stores?

Morales: From our Hispanic Shopper 360 data, we know that U.S. Hispanics find mass merchandise, drug, convenience, and club stores attractive. We also found that supercenters in markets in Texas and Miami are visited frequently by Hispanic shoppers. There's a lot to discover, and concepts such as everyday low pricing (EDLP) are attractive, particularly for those with large families. However, once they are in the store, they need to be able to find what they're looking for and be assured that it's the right product for the job. Because U.S. Hispanics have a lower median income than the overall U.S. population, they cannot afford to make product mistakes. This means the power of known and trusted brands can be a powerful guide in their decision making. However, this does not mean they are not open to other brands, which is why it's essential that investment in building and maintaining brand awareness takes place.

At some point in their acculturation process, they absolutely move to the next level. They will visit a Wal-Mart, a Food 4 Less, or a Target, one of the superstores that doesn't just stock grocery items. That's when difficulties may arise. From a friendly and comforting environment, these new shoppers find themselves in a store with potentially limited recognition of Hispanic consumers as a distinct group. For example, the service staff might not speak the language. The signage and often the packaging will be only in English and they might have difficulty in locating someone who looks like them to ask for advice. The store selection may have limited appeal. As the difficulties mount up, these shoppers end up frustrated by their experience.

None of these obstacles is insurmountable individually, but taken as a whole, they can be formidable. One solution can be to take along someone who speaks English, which is why you often see Hispanics shopping together in groups, but this is not always practical. Retailers can further disrupt the process if they suddenly change the mapping of a store without apparent guidance. In one focus group session, a woman spoke about how she used to frequent Costco and seemed happy with her shopping experience. One day, they changed the location of items she had been familiar with, and she could not find a Hispanic to explain where the items had been moved. As she did not want to feel embarrassed given her English proficiency, she left the store, never to return. She now shops at a store with more visible Hispanic workers to avoid a similar situation. Costco never knew they lost her, or why.

How does this use of many channels affect the way Hispanic shoppers plan to shop?

Morales: You've already talked about how U.S. shoppers in general rarely plan their shopping trips. If anything, this is more of an issue for Hispanics. They shop more frequently than the norm, using the store as a pantry and, therefore, don't see the need to make lists.

In our survey, only 36 percent made and brought shopping lists to the store. Many had a specific brand in mind when they went shopping. So what influences their product choices? There's a lot more word-of-mouth referral for products because that's one of the greatest sources of information, particularly if you're struggling with the language. Store circulars, meanwhile, play a very important role in the shopping process for grocery, drug, and even department stores. About a quarter looked at the store circular. This is a consumer segment that does not do online comparisons as such very often. Instead, they rely on printed material.

One area that has, to date, been under-exploited by retailers is coupons. Currently, they are either not being directed as heavily to Spanish-speaking consumers due to distribution challenges, or go unused due to Hispanics' unfamiliarity with the concept. Moreover, our most recent TNS Hispanic Shopper 360 data also shows that U.S. Hispanics are not major coupon users. In fact, they ranked "I redeem a lot of coupons" very near the bottom of a list of attributes, whereas their general market counterparts ranked this same attribute near the top quartile. Clearly, there are issues of education that would benefit retailer, manufacturer, and the consumer in this area. Sometimes, even if they want to use them or have them in their bag, they just forget—and then the coupons have expired. If this happens on a number of occasions, they get disenchanted with the whole process and will not re-attempt. An additional problem, for those with more limited language proficiency, is the very real fear that they hand a clerk the coupon and then start to receive questions about it. This causes them to stand out or be embarrassed if they have limited language proficiency. As we discussed, culturally, that's not something that they want to do.

In our recent Hispanic Shopper 360 data, we discovered that 65 percent of Hispanics were influenced by in-store offers. This was more than twice the impact of general-market shoppers. So, if coupons seem to have limited appeal, it would make sense to develop and invest in more tactical in-store efforts.

Retailers should also work with manufacturers and community-based organizations to sponsor classes on how to save money or be savvy shoppers that would include both frequent shopper card and coupon use. They could produce printed FAQs in both English and Spanish, which saves money and ensures many potential users.

How does the U.S. Hispanic market react to loyalty cards and other mechanisms to collect customer data?

Morales: We know that growth in many multiples is achieved by learning more about existing customers. The rise of Tesco in the UK, for instance, has been built on the back of the Tesco Clubcard, its loyalty card. In the U.S., however, targeting the Hispanic market in this way is likely to present problems. Loyalty cards are very under-represented in such ethnic groups because of a reluctance to provide personal data and information. The institutional trust that retailers have come to rely on just does not exist and creates a barrier for those who rely on loyalty cards as a tool. In their minds, Hispanics simply want to make their purchase at the best possible price and do not understand why they need to provide the retailer with their personal details to do so. In fact, I would not be surprised to see a similar point of view emerge across the board for shoppers in general, given privacy concerns.

This problem eases further up the acculturation curve, but for those who are new to a country—or who might have entered illegally—giving personal information is a no-go. Even Puerto Ricans, who are U.S. citizens from birth, may be reluctant to do so. Such populations are also likely to opt for unlisted phone numbers—behaviors that make it difficult for retailers to gather valuable data. To compound their problems, Hispanics may borrow cards or get someone else to buy for them—not altogether helpful for a retailer trying to identify patterns of buying behavior. To some extent, this reflects a deep-seated cultural norm related to a sense of distrust of institutions.

How does culture drive shopping behavior?

Morales: Culture plays a critical role in the behavior of multicultural and, for that matter, all consumers. In their excellent book, *Hispanic Marketing*, published in 2005, Felipe Korzenny and Betty Ann Korzenny highlight how marketers need to understand culture to develop deeper emotional connections with Hispanic consumers. Of course, this link to deep cultural understanding applies to all consumers and not simply Hispanics.

In their work, they speak of culture as "the cluster of intangible and tangible aspects of life that groups of humans pass to each other from generation to generation."[1] They use an iceberg as a metaphor for culture, with two aspects: the "objective culture," which appears above the surface, and "subjective culture," which is hidden below the surface.

Foods, music, and clothing are examples of objective culture. In the U.S., the objective culture might include hot dogs and hamburgers, rock and roll, and jeans and t-shirts. For Caribbean Hispanics, these tangible external symbols of culture might include arroz con pollo, salsa, and Guayabera's. Although these external cultural elements are quite different, they are nonetheless highly acceptable and taken-for-granted norms within each culture.

You mentioned the second aspect of culture, subjective culture. How does this affect shopper behavior?

Morales: The second aspect and by far the most important to marketers in my opinion is "subjective culture," a set of beliefs, values, and attitudes that influence how we interact with the world and how the world interacts with us. These aspects are deeply connected to emotions. This emotional connection is exactly where retailers, manufacturers, and all who want to connect with these consumers should focus their efforts. It's not simply that Hispanics tend to have larger families that is important, but rather that your place of business is seen as a welcoming and safe environment where families are welcome and supported with items such as temporary play areas for children, freeing mom to shop at ease.

This notion of connecting to the elements of shoppers' subjective cultural norms and supporting them with objective norms can prove to be a very powerful activator for retailers and marketers. If you have not yet undertaken an exercise to understand the deep emotional connections of your multicultural consumers, it should be a top priority. We will discuss examples later where cultural differences rise to the surface, enabling you to develop products or messaging that appeal to emotional connections.

It is, therefore, essential that before you undertake any serious effort to appeal to multicultural consumers that you truly understand their deeply held beliefs, attitudes, and values. These should guide your development processes whether they are centered on store environment, product development, or advertising and promotion.

In understanding cultures, remember that cultures are not monolithic and will vary even within groups by country of origin. Subjective culture gets to the emotional connection that drives deeply rooted psychological needs. Focus time on deep understanding of beliefs, attitudes, and values of each culture of interest. Then, use these learnings as a touchstone to make investment decisions and guide action.

How does the process of acculturation unfold and what do retailers need to know about it?

Morales: *Acculturation* is the process by which we measure how one culture has adopted the mainstream behaviors of the dominant culture. In the past, it seemed inevitable that people gradually lost touch with their original culture when they put down roots in a new country. However, with significant changes in the thinking about race and ethnicity for many portions of American society, immigrants are no longer forced to adopt the dominant culture. In addition, it is easier than ever before to retain links to homelands. The ability to access print, television, radio, and online media from their country of origin (or at least in their native language) makes it easier to stay connected to their native culture. Our studies found that bilingual Hispanics watched an average of about 3 hours of Spanish television a week (and about 17 hours of English language TV), whereas Spanish-dominant immigrants watched more than 15 hours of Spanish language television (and about 8 hours of English). The presence of large and vibrant support communities also slows the pace of acculturation. Newcomers can subsist quite nicely within relatively small or self-contained communities, continuing to shop at places where they feel comfortable and are welcome. These links may eventually weaken from the first, to the second, and the third generation, but it is a slow and gradual process. My post-election belief is that with an even stronger recognition among these groups, you can have both tight links to your culture and success in America. President Barack Obama is proof positive.

Given the close family relationships in Hispanic culture, how do retailers need to respond?

Morales: Smart retailers latch on to the fact that a welcoming family environment is key. Hispanic Americans tend to shop as families or as groups, and there are often children in tow because the family size/structure is much larger than the median for the U.S. Retailers such as H.E Butt, with its "kid-friendly" zones, have been hailed as a success in marketing to the Hispanic consumer. They have created a tortilleria area, a great concept and very much central to the culture, where they make approximately 10,000 fresh tortillas a day. Bashas, a chain with an

Arizona focus, has also had success with the same type of format. It cares for 6,000+ kids a week at its Cub House while parents shop. All of this contributed to H.E Butt being named "Retailer of the Year" a few years back by Progressive Grocer. Wal-Mart has also been moving in this direction, particularly in Texas, and has even added a Central American chain, Pollo Campero, in some of its stores. It makes it easy to spend lots of time in their stores.

What issues of product selection or packaging do retailers and manufacturers need to address for this segment?

Morales: Planning for a shop can present problems for shoppers who are used to products in one shape or form in their country of origin, yet which have undergone a radical transformation in their new home. They may be familiar with soap and body gel in bar form, for instance, which is now viewed as outdated. Or they may be used to buying laundry powder, when in the U.S., it's the liquid version that is the most popular, for example. They may even be used to seeing much larger packages, instead of more concentrated products in small packages, largely prompted by environmental concerns. So, there are obvious opportunities for retailers and producers to make sure that they're communicating about form, use, and benefits adequately to this population.

There are also product genres that Hispanic shoppers are more likely to avoid, such as frozen food or packaged foods in a box that require microwaving. The culture is still such that it often demands homemade food as it's still essential to mom's pride to care for her family appropriately, and pressure comes from both family and peers. Cooking a meal for your kids shows your love for your family. Hispanic moms are willing to take shortcuts, but only if quality and flavor are not compromised—as with chopped tomatoes for salsa, for example. We know that these barriers start to diminish, however, based on the need of "new" Hispanic moms for convenience and kids' "pester power" and with the length of time in the U.S.

How are companies winning with U.S. Hispanic consumers?

Morales: The companies that have maintained sustained efforts and investment in marketing to immigrant populations are now reaping the benefits. Companies such as Procter & Gamble, for instance, and brands such as Colgate—which is strong in Latin America—have done well. Kraft is another example, as is Heineken, which has seen great growth of late, and McDonald's in the U.S.

The winners win because they have a strategy, stay the course, and invest in their communities. They focus on building awareness, which we have already identified as central to success with this group. Those who invest in building awareness also invest in their various communities through community events, sports sponsorship, music or arts events, and the like. Some have created cookbooks that are Hispanic-themed. Others, such as AT&T on the wireless side, have converted all their stores in Spanish-language areas so that they have a high Spanish-speaking quotient of employees, materials, and advertising. They recognize the importance of "localization" and invest in all areas that are necessary to generate success, applying established marketing principles to these groups, but they do it step by step.

How successful have manufacturers and retailers been in responding to the opportunity of the U.S. Hispanic market segment?

Morales: The Hispanic population has been growing apace, yet retailers woke up relatively late to the potential. It is only now, when the main-stream U.S. population is experiencing virtually as many deaths as births, that they are gearing up for change. In fact, it is manufacturers who are at the forefront—companies such as Procter & Gamble, J&J, Unilever, ConAgra, and so on—who have been very aware of the shifting demographics and are asking retailers what they intend to do to be more welcoming to these consumers. Now there is a dialogue between the two so that they can both benefit. They have in troduced new products that leverage the brand at lower price points. This represents both good business and cultural sensitivity for the early movers.

Different retailers and manufacturers are at different stages in the process, however. Some are more aware than others, and many are putting off investment in this area from one year to the next. In some U.S. cities, meanwhile, traditional grocery stores have been losing out due to Hispanics taking their wallets to dollar stores, and have, therefore, had to adapt. A store like 99, in southern California, which is a supermarket with aisles and aisles of everything from housewares to laundry to food and refrigerated produce—all for $0.99—is a definite incentive for change.

Such change requires investment, though, and not just in store design and signage, but also in providing well-trained individuals who can communicate with shoppers in their language of choice. In fact, hiring, training, and retaining bilingual employees who possess the needed levels of proficiency and customer skills is proving to be a real challenge for many retailers. Providing the right experience for a trust-based consumer is very reliant on this high-touch quotient, and you need to find and retain the right people to achieve success.

Can you give an example of how a retailer or manufacturer has used an understanding of multicultural marketing and U.S. Hispanic markets to build its business?

Morales: La Curacao, a Los Angeles-based department store, is often cited as an example of a retailer that's been very successful in appealing to the Hispanic shopper. Credit is seen as the cornerstone of its success, with the chain catering its credit and other services specifically to the needs of Latino immigrants. It is said to approve 75 percent of credit card applications, whatever the status of applicants, by using unconventional and confidential credit-scoring methods and interviewing techniques.

These cardholders then account for the vast majority of the chain's sales, many of which are consumer electronics, appliances, and furniture. And the card's rate of interest, though higher than some general-market retailers, proved lower than others—a factor that stirred up the market somewhat. It sparked discussions as to what rates should be charged to people who have less knowledge and proficiency in the market than traditional consumers. Nevertheless, all of a sudden, other retailers came under pressure to develop plans focused on the Hispanic marketplace in the U.S.

Another reason for its success is that it has more salespeople per customer than its competitors, although this can impact pricing. High service standards are another factor. As for the store design, it is colorful with Mayan and Aztec architecture and décor, plus it features Spanish-language signs.

Although the chain reflects an astute understanding of the market, it was not founded by Hispanic immigrants. The founders were two brothers who immigrated from Israel in 1997, Jerry and Ron Azarkman. They understood the immigrant experience and built a store to meet the needs of a very different group of immigrants.

You've focused on Hispanic markets in the U.S. How do these insights apply to other markets?

Morales: The learnings are relevant to other countries, and wherever immigration and acculturation is a significant market reality. I recently spoke at a conference in Toronto on "The Changing Face of Shoppers." After the conference, a Middle Eastern banker who now lives in Toronto approached me. He first thanked me for speaking openly about the opportunity multicultural markets represent, which is not widely discussed. He then went on to tell me how Maple Lodge Farms, the largest chicken-processing company in Canada, had focused on the unmet needs of the Muslim community for Halal-certified foods, which are prepared according to strict Muslim religious requirements. These foods were met with great success by the Muslim community in Canada and elsewhere. On their website, you'll find a separate link with great information on the company, process, and its branded Zabiha Halal foods. This is proof positive that if marketers invest the time to understand multicultural consumers' needs, they can profit handsomely by owning the category and establishing a reason to believe from which to introduce new products.

Sometimes the shifts are within the country. China's economic growth, for example, has gone hand in hand with the rapid emergence of a new breed of consumers there: an urban middle class, increasingly sophisticated, with retailers at the sharp end of demands for higher-quality goods and services, variety, and innovation. Yet this retail revolution would not be enough to guarantee inclusion in this chapter. What makes the difference is that there has been an unprecedented migration from rural areas to the cities, which has grown the size of the second- and third-tier urban retail markets. In addition to higher disposable incomes, there has been a trend toward greater ownership of refrigerators (meaning a daily shop is no longer required) and changing lifestyles (working mothers). As for the retailer, local protectionism may well decrease the efficiency of distribution and supply chains, leading to fewer choices or higher prices for consumers.

Still, since China's accession to the World Trade Organization, there has been massive deregulation of the retail and distribution sectors and growth. More than 35 of the top global retailers are now in China. With domestic companies, they are catering to this new rush of consumers to the city. This is a multicultural shift within a single country.[2]

In closing, what would be your top tips for retailers and manufacturers who seek to address multicultural shoppers?

Morales: There are many approaches and subtleties to addressing this market, as we've discussed, but some of the core principles to focus on are the following:

- **Create a comfortable and welcoming shopping environment:** Hispanic shoppers spend more time in stores, often shopping with family, and see the shopping process as entertainment. Comfort is a priority and can be valued over convenience. This can be seen in the ease of shopping (wide aisles, translated signage), kids' play areas, in-store dining options, or even customer service (where warmth and friendliness are key).

- **Understand where these consumers come from:** Learn what experiences they were used to in their countries of origin and what their current values are today to understand the familiarity they seek and how to reach them in a culturally relevant way.

- **Recognize that Hispanic moms want to be smart shoppers:** Give them the opportunity to make smart decisions by providing good value and high-quality products.

- **Cater to the entire family:** Shopping can be a family activity, with children sometimes doing the translating for parents who are less fluent. Provide an environment where all members of the family can shop and enjoy themselves.

- **Go the whole way:** Ensure that multicultural efforts resonate by committing to them entirely. Make sure the customer has cultural/in-language support throughout the shopping process and reinforce the commitment with equally relevant marketing and PR efforts.

- **Make education a priority:** These consumers often are unfamiliar with brands or even entire product categories. Make sure to give the explanation of how products work and ideas on ways to use them. In terms of in-store policies (returns, exchanges, loyalty cards, and so on), explain how they work to create a greater sense of trust and comfort. Remember that multicultural shoppers might be uncomfortable about embarrassing themselves by asking.

- **Develop a holistic multicultural marketing strategy:** If you already have a strategy, check to be sure it's still relevant and delivering on its promise. If it's off target, spend the time to find out why and how to get it back on track.

- **Don't fear in-language communications:** Research shows that the vast majority of consumers don't care if your communications and packaging are in two languages. It is becoming a "taken for granted." Also bear in mind that if it works for today's market leaders, it should also work for you.

- **Get out there:** Don't simply rely on reports or the occasional focus groups (although they are both useful). Go out and meet with a few of the more than 46 million U.S. Hispanic shoppers (or African-American or Asian shoppers). It will absolutely change your thinking about the potential of these markets for your business.

Endnotes

1. Korzenny, Felipe and Korzenny, Betty Ann. *Hispanic Marketing: A Cultural Perspective.* Elsevier Butterworth-Heinemann, Oxford, UK. 2005.

2. ChinaRetailNews.com. "Investing in China's Retail Industry," April 2006, PriceWaterhouseCoopers.

9

Insights into Action: A Retailer Responds: *An Interview with Mark Heckman of Marsh Supermarkets*

T he research and insights of this book were tested in the crucible of the supermarket aisle, but we turn now to an experienced retailer to reflect more deeply on how these approaches can be put into action. In this closing interview, Mark Heckman, vice president of marketing of Marsh Supermarkets, discusses how he took the insights of the book into the trenches of retail. Marsh, which was the first grocery store in the world to use electronic scanners to ring up purchases, operates more than 100 supermarkets in Indiana and Ohio.

What are the most important things to keep in mind when implementing changes in the retail format, such as those described in this book?

Heckman: It's a "walk, don't run" environment. Pick out a couple of things to try. For most retailers, it isn't going to be a revolutionary process. It's going to be an evolutionary process. We try to get some small wins at first. We try to keep a few simple things in mind when we design these stores. You need to keep the front ends open and free; you need to make sure that there are a lot of different options for shoppers to diffuse themselves throughout the store. Design a right-hand store whenever you can, as opposed to a left-hand store. Make sure the displays in the aisles are facing toward the rear because most of the traffic is coming from the back to the front. In one store, we removed a "stock-up" center aisle that created a barrier to the center of the store. By taking out this obstacle, we improved the flow of shoppers into the center.

Pay attention to operations. We try to keep our layouts pretty clean; we don't junk them up with shippers and other kinds of displays that an awful lot of retailers do. I think when you talk about the way a store is laid out with its permanent fixtures, its gondolas and its end caps, and its departments, sometimes a very clean and workable layout can be rendered totally useless by poor operations clogging up aisles.

It's amazing to me that after we built a few new stores based on these concepts, I'm starting to see people using these principles as conventional knowledge. It doesn't have to be revolutionary changes. It can just be: Use these basic principles and just prove to yourself that they work because they will. You are not going to turn the world upside down overnight. You are looking for incremental advantages.

What have been the results in the stores you've redesigned?

Heckman: These stores have achieved double-digit sales increases. We have seen increased penetration of private label and center of store categories, and increased overall basket size. The stores have also done well on qualitative measures. Customer satisfaction and intent to return have both increased. At the same time, the exposure of pallet drops and end caps have sustained our low-price image.

How are retailers beginning to implement new designs, such as serpentine or inverted perimeter approaches (discussed in Chapter 3)?

Heckman: Some supermarkets are trying to invert their stores a bit to get more activity into the center of the store, to populate some of those categories that aren't getting as much attention as they used to. In some cases, this is because fewer people are buying those categories, because of consumer trends. In most cases, there are so many other kinds of retailers selling those categories that the supermarkets do not dominate those categories the way they used to. I would also tell you that trying to classify formats gets tied very neatly into different kinds of retailers that are available to the consumer. The retailer is starting to look at a supermarket differently or use it differently than before.

How do retailers decide whether to take new approaches?

Heckman: I think one of the things that are pushing stores to provide a little bit more of a quick, more convenient shop is the fact that they can't win at being the biggest. You can't be all things. I think retailers like Marsh and others have figured out that we shouldn't try to be the biggest. We should try to be the most convenient or the fastest or whatever that "-est" is. So, I think that's driving us to look at our stores a little differently because consumers are looking at us in a different light than they used to.

When you talk about the retailer that can pull off a serpentine store, I think it has to be a lot more unique and a lot more of a specialty orientation than other stores because it would only attract a shopper who is prepared to browse. That format would actually be conducive to success only for a shopper who can spend time to really sniff the roses, so to speak. I think it works at Stew Leonard's and Central Market because the shoppers have a more casual mindset when they come into those stores.

In my opinion, what supermarkets are doing is trying what works willy-nilly. You are going to get a lot more tweaking of what works than you are radical departures. What do you think?

Heckman: This is where it is important to have stores within stores—what you are calling the "compound store." If the compound store is successful, I think then the next question is: Where are these departments vis-à-vis each other, and what is the optimal layout of the departments? Then you almost have two sets of dynamics. You've got the overall positioning of the stores within a store and then what happens to the customers when they get in those stores within a store. How do they shop, and how is that different depending upon what the category is or where the store is or where that department is?

At Marsh, are you moving in the direction of an inverted store (as discussed in Chapter 3)?

Heckman: We have done some things of that nature. We have two stores that are called "circle stores." Essentially, we have inverted those stores in relationship to where the classic departments are in a perimeter-oriented store. We've taken most of the perishables and the *theater* of the store, and we've put it right front and center in the middle of the building. We then pushed all the aisle departments, the traditional center store departments, into perimeter shops, categorized by the function of that shop, such as household cleaning, frozen foods, meat, or dairy. Those kinds of things are in alcoves. The center of the store focuses on produce, international foods, the varieties, the organics, and those kinds of things. People really have an opportunity to see the specialty nature of that format, and that can be the draw. If they need to go into any of those perimeter departments, they know where to go because those are smartly called out. With that said, it took customers a long time to figure this out.

How do shoppers react to these new formats?

Heckman: It was such a radical departure from how they were shopping in any other supermarket, or any other Marsh store for that matter, it took time. Once they have gone through a three- or four-month period where they stay with you, they start to like it. As a matter of fact, our sales in those two stores have dramatically jumped up without really any improvement or any adjustment in the layout. It's just a matter of consumers getting comfortable. Customers that do shop those stores actually say they like it better because it helps them stay on task. Once customers learn the store, there is not only a lift, but also it actually becomes an exit barrier. Once they learn the store, they like the store, and it becomes a positive point of differentiation for them.

On the other hand, retailers want to promote that incremental shop, that incremental item in the basket. We haven't done a lot of detailed empirical work on this, but we have found out that our basket size is still fairly large because they're in areas that are conducive for large basket shopping. Our concern there is that we just don't get as much impulse shopping because we have compartmentalized things.

Those formats got quite a bit of press when they were first launched back in 2002 or 2003. We've decided not to build any more of those. First of all, we haven't been building a great many new stores, period. We've been upgrading and remodeling the ones we have. But we also felt that format was just too radical for folks to make the adjustment. We were just afraid that, because retailers need such an immediate return on their investment, we didn't have the time. If we were a Stew Leonard's or we even had the reputation of an HEB Central Market for specialty, we could probably get away with those kinds of formats.

Shoppers will hang in there to learn the new store formats?

Heckman: Exactly. And again one could weigh the merits of the fact that maybe they're not impulse buying as much as they would in other formats. But if it attracts customers, and it increases your customer count, perhaps you could drive your business without thinking you have to cross-merchandise these departments as heavily as we do in some of the other stores.

Are you comfortable with the idea that customers become shoppers only within the walls of the store?

Heckman: As long as you include what goes on in the vestibule. There's another initiative going on with the folks that manage all the things that happen on the other side of the checkout. They call it the "fifth wall." You've got four walls where they shop for groceries. Now there's a fifth wall where there's a place to get your DVDs, change your coins into cash, use an ATM, or those kinds of things. But clearly within the four walls, a consumer becomes a shopper; there's no dispute about that.

You've looked a lot at pre-shopping, which we have not considered in the book. How do people decide what store to shop at, and what kind of metrics do you look at outside the store?

Heckman: We do know how folks select stores, and that varies somewhat from big box formats to more traditional formats, all the way down to convenience stores. The dynamics change for each one of those kinds of stores. Consumers look for geographically convenient *rooftops*. In urban areas, there typically are three or four supermarkets for every three or four square miles just because there is a demand for that many. You try to put yourself in a "first right of refusal" position to as many conveniently located households as possible. The first right of refusal's very important in our business, and that means that you drive by us either coming from work, going to work, or coming from home to anywhere you go. You have to drive by us to get to somebody else. We feel like if we have first right of refusal to, say, 60 percent of the geographically convenient trade, then if we get our fair share of that—and our fair share is the lion's share—then that store has a chance to be successful. If you're not getting your fair share of that business, you're probably going to have a problem with that store because that means they're rejecting you, even though you're more convenient to them.

Now, convenience means a lot of different things. It can mean that I'm driving by you and it's only a mile from my house, where brand X is two miles from my house. Convenience also means that I can get into your shopping center easily. I can get in and out without spending an hour doing so. The parking lot is laid out well; it's safe, clean, and well lit at night. Upscale people tend to shop in upscale locations; they don't necessarily like to drive into areas that aren't on par with where they live. But more downscale or midscale shoppers don't mind shopping up. They're more likely to do that than the other way around.

Can you shed some light on what are the half dozen most important metrics you use?

Heckman: The most obvious ones are measurements of sales volume, but we also look at item count. Particularly in times of inflation, you want to make sure that your business isn't being driven by just inflation as opposed to items being purchased. So, we look at item counts and average unit price. We measure dollars per square foot and sales area per square foot to talk about how productive our stores are relative to how big they are. That's a metric that a lot of the industry uses to normalize production between chains. Nielsen certainly uses that metric a lot to extrapolate sales volumes. The other big number that most retailers look at is comparative store sales or same store sales year on year. We also look at overall gross margins and our bill out.

One measure we are using is how many seconds it takes for each store to generate a dollar of sales. They run anywhere from 30 seconds to 120 per dollar. What do you think about this measure?

Heckman: It would be a very useful measure if you could effect change and remeasure it to see if you are making headway.

Do you have your own shopper segmentation scheme at Marsh?

Heckman: We do segment our shoppers by their spending and frequency. We have a loyalty card, and we have identified loyal elites, infrequent and occasional shoppers, and a couple of other classifications. We don't have to infer. We can look at coupon usage or we can look at the percentage of sale items that populate a particular shopper's basket, and we can segment against that. If we are going to communicate to a couple of groups of shoppers, if one is going to be more price sensitive than the other, we'll communicate to those folks a little differently than we might communicate to another group. Brands take a different tack. They might want to talk to a retailer's best shoppers just because these shoppers are in the store more often and more likely to see the offer. Beyond that, they differentiate between loyalists and switchers. We also target life stages—college students, moms with kids, or senior citizens.

Retailers do not have a lot of time or a lot of firepower to devote to this. We don't have a team of horses to put on projects. I'd like to have a person who was dedicated to managing two or three customer segments. So, we do the best we can. With loyalty cards, the bar is now too high. If it's just about discounts, it's very difficult to engender loyalty through your card.

Are you doing something distinctly to serve quick trippers?

Heckman: We are. We certainly offer categories of products that are conducive for shoppers to come in, get their meals for that evening, and get out quickly. We do not have them consolidated in a quick-trip store within a store. Some retailers have gone to the point where you're walking into almost a convenience store inside their store. We do have convenience areas toward the front of the store, and that's particularly true in our larger stores. But they aren't necessarily positioned so that they're right next to the home meal replacement center or they're right next to categories of products that people tend to buy on short trips.

Is there a brand/retailer partnership?

Heckman: Brands have figured out that if they get a display in the store, almost any promotion they run with that retailer pays out because of the incremental lift they get from the exposure to display. It really goes right back to the principles that you've been preaching for a number of years that you have to get that conversion process.

Brands have got to reach the shopper. The preponderance of people stay on the perimeter of the store. If you can get a display in the store, and brands know this, they'll pay a premium for that, and they basically wrap up almost all of their promotions around the concept.

Retailers tend, almost to a fault, to let manufacturers dominate their stores with displays just because manufacturers have figured out that's what drives their sales, and so they're ready to pay the retailer almost real estate rental for different end caps. We have a number of different contracts throughout our store. If you walk through our store, you'll see fixed end caps and fixed displays, and the same thing holds true for almost any major retailer in the country. You see Wal-Mart doing it with various brands. Target's been doing it for years with brands of clothing. That kind of exposure gets the sales that brands need. I think there's been some progress made where retailers and brands have figured out a way to get along and to mutually benefit. But when it comes down to what the brands' ultimate objectives are and the retailers' ultimate objectives are, the brand wants to sell more of their own products, and the retailer wants to sell more of that category's product. It's only when those two objectives converge is when you have success.

A very progressive company did some research that showed shoppers don't like to put heavy things on top of light things. That was their total focus. But if shoppers pick up the product early on, then I've got nothing else to sell these folks in the store. What happens if folks don't shop the entire store; what happens to the efficiency of my displays if the category is presented early? They didn't think through any of that. They just kept it on a very singular train: "Shoppers told us this, so let's do it." There's so much more to it than that.

What shoppers tell us is sometimes a very poor source?
Heckman: They lie to you sometimes. They can't tell you, but they can show you.

I think shoppers would love to spend a lot more money in stores, but they can't figure out how to do it. I think there's a huge amount of unfulfilled shopping out there. What do you think?
Heckman: I do think that's true. I don't think a shopper has a conscious mindset that says: "I'll be disappointed if I don't spend a lot of money here." I think most shoppers are consciously thinking that they want to

be able to save money. Even the most affluent folks like to save. But at the same time, if you offer them something, if they see something that strikes their fancy, it's a lot more fun. You never hear anybody get back from the store and say: "I went to the store today, and I bought everything on my list. Wow, was that fun!" They usually say: "I went to the store today, and I got everything on my list, but there were three things I didn't expect. They had salmon on sale or they had something that looked so good I had to have it." It's always about that incremental purchase, something that has invoked their sensory program, something they weren't expecting that made their shopping trip successful.

The clubs are successful because they do have the element of: What do you have today that you didn't have yesterday? Traditional retailers can do that as well with promotion and visual merchandising.

What are you doing with new technologies?

Heckman: We are doing text messaging, and we are certainly doing an awful lot online to help the shopper prepare for their trip from the website. We use text messaging to send them the top offers. As we evolve that program, eventually it will be customized offers. Shoppers are relying a lot more on online and electronic programs to help them prepare themselves so that once they get to the store, they can be as efficient as possible. Some programs, for example, help shoppers prepare their lists by putting the items in the order of how they'll encounter the products in the store. We're trying to do that, and we've had an awful lot of requests for that. Making the store shopable doesn't have to begin at the store. It can begin online by getting somebody to look at the ad online before they get to the store. We've set up a special website for a brand-new store where you can look at the store map and you can look at different photographs of the different displays in the areas of the store. You can get a feel of the store even before you walk in.

PART III

Conclusions

10

The Internet Goes Shopping

"To change and improve are two different things."

—German proverb

In Chapter 7, "Integrating Online and Offline Retailing," we discussed with Peter Fader and Wendy Moe the similarities between online and offline shopping behavior. We saw how insights from e-commerce can be applied in brick-and-mortar stores. But the online and offline worlds are converging in a more direct sense through new technologies for interacting with shoppers inside the store. While consumers have gone online to shop, now the Internet is coming into the physical shopping experience. Although we are still in the early stages of this evolution, neither world will ever be the same.

There is a long history of wanting to communicate with shoppers while they are shopping in brick-and-mortar stores, but the early efforts were rather crude. Retailers placed fixed advertising and communications around the store that was contextually sensitive—placing coupons on or near the product, or near a logically related product, for example. But the true goal has long been to communicate with a specific shopper in a particular location and change the message dynamically as the shopper moves through the store (even, perhaps, influencing the shopper's path). This would provide messages that are relevant to that shopper at a specific point in her trip in a specific store.

Entering the VideoCart Age

Online-offline retail fusion began with VideoCart and evolved to the present diverging approaches—a full cart system such as MediaCart with a large screen and Internet connection or a handheld device such as Modiv Media's. Let's take a quick look at this evolution.

VideoCart was developed in the early 1990s by marketing research company Information Resources, Inc. (IRI), which sells family grocery-buying statistics to clients such as Procter & Gamble and Nabisco. VideoCart, the world's first Internet business-to-consumer start-up, operated over 20,000 carts in more than 200 U.S. grocery and chain retailers by 1992. The carts had battery-operated mobile displays about the size of an Etch A Sketch™ mounted on their handles, connected to the company's servers through wireless LANs in stores. The interactive displays received completely new content via download every week, because prices change weekly in grocery stores, including sale items and coupons for that unique store (the same information as in the local newspaper's weekly food section). Each device was location-sensitive, displaying only the on-sale items in the shoppers' immediate vicinity, and changing as they went down the aisle or entered another department.

Other pilot sites for VideoCart included Wal-Mart and Toys-R-Us. The content, or weekly "show," included what may have been the first banner ads, with animation. Coupons and banner ads were similarly location-specific. The device had an ATM screen-with-buttons, the only public digital interface then in common use, which provided coupons at checkout. The Videocart devices also offered entertainment to shoppers in the checkout line.[1] The most advanced systems logged all shopping cart paths and could analyze and play back individual or aggregate paths through a store map. Ultimately, this tied the path data, time-of-day, and day-of-week to effectiveness of sales, coupons, or shelf-placement.

That effort was followed by the less successful ActivityPath, and later, Magellan by Safeway. Stop & Shop has been the most persistent retailer pressing this opportunity, first with Shopping Buddy, with a full-size interactive screen on the cart, which has evolved into a handheld device (Modiv Media). Modiv Media now is operating in more than 100 stores, so it has moved well beyond proof of concept to demonstrate the value of this approach. Building on VideoCart's success, MediaCart now offers a computerized shopping cart that assists shoppers, delivers targeted communications at the point of purchase, and streamlines store operations. The MediaCart system accurately anticipates and responds to shopping needs—letting shoppers download a shopping list from home, plot the quickest and easiest route around the store, locate products, check prices, and scan and bag their items seamlessly while shopping. The system uses passive RFID tracking of the cart through the store and WiFi radio signals to the store's central servers. Shoppers can press a button to ask where a product is and locate the best route there. When the product is selected, the shopper scans the barcode on the screen, and it is added to the total for the cart.

Cell Phone Invasion

So far, most of the tracking and interaction in stores requires specialized devices, either bulky "laptops" mounted on carts or handheld devices. But as iPhones and other powerful cell phones become more ubiquitous, they will play an increasingly important role in interacting with shoppers in the store. Phones already track their locations relative to cell towers and GPS systems. There are RFID reader chips going into cell phones that will permit location-specific communication with shoppers in the aisles of stores. This is not the same as VideoCart, Modiv Shopper, or MediaCart, but it could mean that consumers will carry their connection to retail stores in their own pockets.

Ten years from now, retailers will be communicating with shoppers on a regular basis as they walk around the store using some kind of electronic device, whether it's their cell phone, PDA, or equipment the retailer provides. All retailing will occur under this cloud of electronic communication. This will promote more active participation with the shopper, taking us closer to what I have called the Holy Grail of retailing:

- To know exactly what each shopper wants, or might buy, as they come through the front door

- To deliver that to them right away, accepting their cash quickly and speeding them on their way

The bottom line is that the Internet is moving into the store, which will fully blend online and offline retailing. Retailing itself will be altered to a great extent by this. The offline store will increasingly become a "big head" enterprise (think Stew Leonard's, HEB Central Market, and Tesco's Fresh & Easy). But Chris Anderson's vision of the "long tail" will take on added relevance, as, for example, supermarkets learn to distinctly manage their center-of-store long tails versus their promotional big head stores.

The wired store may also enable the long tail to hang outside the four walls of the store. This is where Internet maestros like Tesco may sweep a few dinosaurs into the dustbin of history. However, all the largest players are already working both sides of the street (online/offline) and will eventually figure out that pushing 30,000 SKUs into shoppers' faces every time they show up in the "store," when they only buy 200 regularly, is killing their business. (I look at the $20 million of sales of a good supermarket as "death" compared to Stew Leonard's $100 million per store.)

The shifting relationship between the shopper and retailer is bound to further disturb their relationship with the third leg of this stool, the brand owners. Manufacturers and retailers will need to examine their relationship to see if their current systems for interacting, such as a trillion dollars in promotional fees, really serve shoppers well—or any of the three parties in this emerging world. Already these relationships are starting to change to meet the demands of a more shopper-centric world, where shoppers are king and queen. As King Louis discovered many years ago in France, it is hard to hold back such a tide of change. No matter what the current powers may think, these shoppers will not "eat cake"— unless they absolutely want to.

Implications for Retailers and Brand Owners

The primary message of our research for retailers is to *manage the big head and long tail* of in-store products more effectively. This will help you make better use of the 80 percent of shopper time that is wasted moving through the thousands of products in the store to get to the few hundred that shoppers actually purchase. There are many possible solutions, but retailers that don't know how to manage the big head and long tail will not be in business long. As noted previously, online retailing offers opportunities for many new and creative solutions to this challenge.

For brand owners, the key is to improve the *speed of closing*. Although the retailers may control how the shopper moves through the store, the manufacturer influences the speed of closing when the shopper is within striking distance of the product. In addition to packaging, in-store digital media can help to close the sale. If brand owners want to significantly increase their sales, they need to engage with the shopper in real-time conversation through digital media at the point where the purchase is made. This significantly speeds up seconds per dollar, which, as we've discussed, increases overall sales. Brands need to make relevant, timely offers and close the deal quickly.

The Power of Model Makers

New technologies not only create more opportunities to interact with shoppers but also are a rich source of new information to help us understand shopper behavior. As noted previously, smart shopping carts can track consumer pathways through the store and offer insights into their reactions to specific displays or promotions along the way. These are the kind of tools that we only dreamed about having a few decades ago. As we have found with scanners and online clickstreams, however, massive amounts of data do not necessarily lead to better insights. Wharton's Peter Fader has commented that much of the experimentation online is *atheoretical*. People manipulate pages and see what works, but don't use the results to inform a broader theory.

Even in an environment that is so rich in information and offers so many channels for potential interaction as the one emerging, there will be a need to understand shopper behavior. Given that humans are still at the center of this drama and their needs and behaviors are often resistant to the tug of new technology, our past insights into how shoppers behave, as described in this book, are likely to remain very relevant in this new era. It is encouraging to see the research discussed in Chapter 7 about the parallels between online and offline behavior, which shows that while there are important differences, shoppers are shoppers.

In fact, insights and theories about shopper behavior may be even more important in our high-tech environment. If you can interact with shoppers at every moment during their trip, and in many different ways, how do you interact in just the right way? This is similar to online advertising where it may be *possible* to bombard a visitor to a site with a barrage of popup ads—possible, but probably not desirable. A strategy for where and when and how to interact with shoppers becomes crucial. And a solid strategy rests on solid theory tested with empirical results. That is where good models come in.

The Model Business

Online or offline, models matter. The movie *The Flight of the Phoenix* tells the story of an airplane that crashes in the desert, in time of war. With enemies all around, the survivors have no way to fly their damaged plane. It appears that they will perish in the hot desert through exposure and lack of food and water. But, as chance would have it, among the survivors is an aircraft design engineer with many years experience. He suggests that they can make some fundamental changes in the remains of the plane, and this "new" plane can fly them out of their peril. At the last instant before their lifesaving flight, they learn that their aeronautical design engineer has spent his entire career *designing model airplanes*! He is a model maker. Yet they managed to take off and fly to safety.

I have also been a model maker, but am just as confident in the knowledge we have gained from this process. I am grateful to the many retailers and brands who placed their lives—or at least their livelihoods—into the hands of our researchers. The knowledge we have gained has helped them and others improve their stores and lift their sales.

This book is the distillation of nearly forty years of a scientist spending time in stores studying shoppers, with the last decade increasingly spent on understanding the relationship of those shoppers to the store and its management, on the one hand, and to the products and their brand suppliers on the other. During the sixteen years immediately preceding the sale of my own company to a global research and information business, we grew at an annualized rate of 30 percent. I don't need to brag, but you need to understand that I do have somewhat of a single-minded focus on growth.

A Fivefold Increase

As with the survivors of *The Phoenix*, attitude is everything. Attitude at retail is a factor given too little consideration, when a large share of achievement is attitude. The reason many people accomplish very little is that they set out to accomplish very little. Actually, people often *start out* with big ideas, but long before they are anywhere near achievement, they have really, totally forgotten what it was they were going to do.

This book has identified the principles that have allowed retailers to increase sales by a factor of five. These retailers understood better what was going on inside the black box of retail. This should be of interest to any retailer or brand owner. And if you fall short of a fivefold increase in sales, wouldn't you be impressed if you could double your sales? The opportunities are there, but you need the right insights and attitude to seize them.

Endnotes

1. http://www.dodsworth.com/videocart.html

11

Game-Changing Retail: A Manifesto

In the months since completing the draft of this book, I have seen growing interest in the practical application of the findings reported here to the opportunities at retail. This manifesto is a distillation of critical action points that will lead to double-digit sales and profit increases, and which have actually led some retailers to achieve as much as *five times* more sales over the past many years.

The adage, "The good is the enemy of the great," is possibly nowhere more applicable than in retailing. With a global population nearing seven billion, the world demand for goods and services is swelling. The movement from developing societies (traditional retailing) to highly developed societies (modern retailing) continues apace. *Demand* alone has been the driving force behind *good* retailing, globally.

A striking feature of good retailing has been almost a single-minded focus on matching the right selection of merchandise to the customer base, with little or no regard to the *time* it costs shoppers to acquire the merchandise. Good retailers, with their suppliers' complicity, regularly squander (waste) 80 percent of the shopper's time. Great retailers will make productive use of that "lost" time.

A new movement in retailing will *change the global game*. The principles outlined next are listed roughly in terms of urgent priority for those who aspire to survive and thrive when their competition is not simply good, but *great*! In most cases, the advance is one of recognizing important distinctions, and responding appropriately, and distinctly, rather than leaving it to shoppers to sort it out for themselves. Although all of these principles are relevant to both retailers and their brand suppliers, the first five deserve the greatest attention by retailers, whereas the last five are most relevant to suppliers:

1. **Focus on the short trip.** For supermarkets around the world (the same principle applies to *all* classes of trade), half of all shopping trips result in the purchase of five or fewer items, with one being the most common. These short trips typically account for one-third of store sales. The *new strategy* is to increase the size of each of those baskets by one or two items. Quick trippers spend money *very* fast, and getting them to buy one or two more items is far easier than motivating stock-up shoppers to buy ten or twenty more items. This focus, focus, focus on the quick trip could deliver an easy 30 percent sales lift (and a lot more when the synergies with other types of trips become apparent).

2. **Focus on the "vital few"** *items* **that drive success.** Fewer than 1,000 items, and perhaps as few as 100 to 200, make the difference between good retailing and great retailing. Which ones are they? Just as the store transaction log tells how many items are in each shopper's basket (Focus 1), it also identifies the *exact* items. Dump all the baskets together, sort them by item (SKU, UPC, EAN, PLU, and so on), count each item, and rank them from the highest selling to the least sold. Your shoppers are voting every day for what they want to buy. Good retailers don't know (or don't care) about this, but great retailers do. Good retailers are obsessed about what they (and their suppliers) want to sell to shoppers. Great retailers are obsessed about what shoppers want to buy!

3. **Display the "vital few" (or the "big head")** *along the dominant path your shoppers take,* **rather than expecting them to find them.** Good retailers expect shoppers to find the merchandise they want; great retailers learn all they can about what the shoppers want, and *take it to them!* This, of course, presupposes some modicum of understanding of the shopper's dominant path. Good retailers are unsure; great retailers have this down pat. Points #2 and #3 are components of the new science of *item management,* a far-sharper instrument than the category management used by all good retailers. Point #3 distinguishes high-value real estate, within the store, from the rest.

4. **The most important promotion is place,** *not* **price.** In a typical store, probably 2 percent of the total items in the store at any one time are being promoted on end-of-aisle displays or other

secondary promotional displays. This 2 percent of items may constitute a full 30 percent of all the sales in the store. However, half the shoppers purchasing an item from one of these promotional displays are unaware that it is at a reduced price. Of the half who are aware, half of those really didn't care about the price. Good retailers are locked in a mindset that price considerations dominate shopping. Great retailers realize that there are other currencies that matter to shoppers in addition to money (time and angst). Great retailers focus on value and convenience: Convenience means fast, *fast*, FAST! Using less of the shopper's time will lead to *more* sales. Hence, Sorensen's primary principle of retail sales is *the faster you sell, the more you will sell.*

5. **Open space attracts!** Shoppers compete with products for space in the store. Good retailers might be oblivious to this competition, and freely tip the balance in favor of the products over the shoppers. Jamming the store with products leads to lots of narrow aisles ("aisleness") and psychic discomfort for shoppers. Great retailers refuse to sacrifice shopper space, and use wide promenades to lead *crowds* of shoppers through a speedy, efficient, high-dollar trip. The allocation of open space is of paramount importance in store design—and there is no single recipe for success.

The following five principles are more closely aligned with the concerns of brand suppliers:

6. **Balance the role of your store's vital few with the rest of your extensive line.** Keep offering the "long tail," but make it easier for the shopper to reach the "big head." Although the sales of the "other" 30,000+ items, the "long tail," do add up to significant sales and profits in aggregate, on an individual basis they are not terribly consequential in total sales. They play a far different and distinct role: Shoppers are attracted to the store by the long tail, but when they get there, they buy the big head (the vital few). The 50 million books Amazon carries encourages me to think they will probably have the few a month that I want. But they would be out of business (I think) if each time I came through their virtual door, they started from scratch to identify what I most likely want to buy. This is the challenge at *all* retail stores, whether online or offline: How to have a huge product selection (very attractive to shoppers) without suppressing sales

by burying the vital few in that massive selection? The key is *distinction*, so that the shopper can immediately reach and recognize the vital few.

7. **Paying to get your own vital few into favorable placement within the store makes sense, depending on the "reach" of the location.** To make a sale, you must reach the shopper with the product; then the product must stop shoppers; and then you close the sale. As noted in point #4, place is more important than price. In fact, charging cut prices at high-value promotional locations devalues both the real estate and the brand. *Selective* price promotion would be more appropriate for long tail items displayed in-aisle, and particularly for those items that are closest in sales rank to the vital few.

8. **Focus on the vital few within your brand, and that of your competition.** Some of your own vital few will not make it into the retailers' vital few. Just as retailers can more readily obtain double-digit sales increases for their vital few, so you can more easily turn your top few sellers into super performers than bring up the laggards. Again, long tail principles apply—the long tail attracts, and the vital few sells. Maintaining a reasonable long tail is essential for both attractive purposes, as well as the competitive imperative. Make clear distinctions in your planning and thinking on these issues.

9. **Reach you can buy, but stopping power and closing power are inherent to the product, primarily through the package.** Both stopping power and closing power can be measured for individual products, as well as categories. The significance is that some products are good at attracting attention, but poor at closing the sale, whereas others are good at closing, but can't seem to stop the traffic. Besides remedial package design, appropriate shelf management and promotional strategies can increase the stopping and closing power of existing products.

10. **Stores have massively excessive verbal communication. Products and packaging are a significant part of the clutter.** Using iconic images, colors, shapes, and appropriate emotional totems is a better way to connect to shoppers than more words. Using category reinvention, you can upgrade the emotional feel of an entire aisle or department. The coffee aisle, for example, can be

redesigned to give it a café ambiance. Remember, the goal is to make your winners win bigger. This will be more easily done with large displays that you can dominate—appropriate to your vital few. And now on the near and far horizon, digital media, even interactive, is a tool of greatest value to you as the brand owner. This means that you can win even in good retailers. Great retailers will expect and appreciate your cooperation with game-changed retailing!

These are just a few of the principles that can be extracted from the research that informs this book. Although these general principles hold across many retail settings and types of products, precise solutions need to be tailored to the specific context. Above all, *great* retailers and brand owners continue to experiment. They test to find out what works, and what doesn't, so they can continue to improve their strategies. This rigorous investigation and testing is how we arrived at the principles discussed previously. Good retailers and brand suppliers, on the other hand, stick with the tried-and-true conventional wisdom. But as the world changes through new technologies, consumer shifts, and new competitors, the great retailers and brand suppliers create the new conventional wisdom and tailor it precisely to their own situations. In that context, the preceding ten points represent an initial hypothesis for this process of ongoing experimentation.

PART IV

Appendix

Appendix

Views on the World of Shoppers, Retailers, and Brands

A pioneer of in-store research, the late Bob Stevens of Procter & Gamble offered a newsletter that he called "Views from the Hills of Kentucky," where he provided perspectives on shopping. Inspired by Bob, I've recently started my own online column in the spirit of his messages, which I've called "Views" as a tribute to his earlier work. In this Appendix, I've selected two excerpts from his columns that remain highly relevant to understanding shopping to give you a taste of his work. I encourage you to visit our archive of his wonderful columns at http://www.tns-sorensen.com/views/archive/views/. To see my latest "Views" entries on our ongoing studies of in-store retailing, please see http://www.insidethemindoftheshopper.com/.

Excerpts from "Views from the Hills of Kentucky" by Robert Stevens

Testers Versus Users

When asked to test something, do you

- Look at and use it differently than when you just happen to be using the same item?
- See things that you would not normally see in the course of using the same product?
- Look more closely at the physical characteristics of the product?
- Look more closely at the packaging?
- Think performance features take on different meanings?

If you answered "Yes" to most, if not all, of the preceding, you are a typical user and tester. Research has found that when you ask a person to test something for you, they place it under the microscope. They see things that, in the course of normal usage, they would never see or even consider.

If the preceding is true, how is it that almost all research is conducted in the test environment? It would seem to me that we would have some interest in the user environment, especially if there is a substantial difference in the assessment under the two perspectives. We don't, after all, sell to the world's testers but to users. It is they who dictate a brand's success or failure.

Actually, I like using both the tester and the user environment when assessing a brand's potential. I generally prefer to use testers in the upstream research and, as I get closer to market, I use the user perspective.

I have found that very few companies use the latter when assessing a brand's potential. Why? I think that few companies realize that two perspectives exist. Among those who do, many don't use the users because few field services offer both options, and it is perceived to be difficult and expensive. I've never found that to be so, but it does, however, take organization and skill to execute properly.

I wonder how many really good ideas are killed in the testing phase because they are being scrutinized so closely, whereas, if the problem appeared in the market, it would never be considered or even seen.

I'm reminded of an experiment in researching the effects of a test protocol in the late 1960s. We were about to conduct a CLT recall of a laundry detergent test among 360 female heads-of-household.

We also had a hand dishwashing detergent study cancel. From the cancelled study, we had 240 blind samples of a current market product. We divided the returning laundry detergent users into two panels, odd- and even-numbered.

After the laundry detergent interview was completed, we asked the even-numbered panelists (120 of them) if they would like to participate in another test. Those who said "Yes" were given a bottle of the dishwashing detergent and were told we would call them in two weeks to conduct the interview.

For the odd-numbered panelists, we told them we had some leftover dishwashing detergent and did not want to send it back to the plant. If they wanted a bottle, they could have one.

After two weeks, both panels were called and interviewed. The results of the study showed dramatic differences in the responses between the odd- and even-numbered panels. Those who were asked to "test" the dish-washing detergent responded in much greater detail than those who were "given" a leftover sample.

Is there a right and wrong protocol? No. I believe there is a time and a place for both types of research. Both approaches bring valuable data to the table. It is important to know when to use each approach. I also expect that the difference between the two panels will be a function of the test product's quality, where excellent and poor products will show bigger differences between panels, while average products will result in smaller differences.

Assessment in Context

Here, I'll outline the results of four in-store packaging studies. The results of three of the studies indicated that the projects should move forward into the market, whereas conventional studies indicated that the projects should not move forward. The results of the fourth study indicated that the project should not move forward, whereas the conventional testing said the project should go forward. In all four cases, the management of the sponsoring companies followed the guidance from the in-store research.

Case Study #1: Package Outage Problem

A new process for making a product was about to be introduced into the market. The warehouse physical properties measurements of the product uncovered an unusual amount of outage (empty space above the product in the container). Quickly, consumer tests were conducted. The results concluded that in no way should this product go to the market. An in-store consumer test of the product was conducted, with the results indicating that the product was highly acceptable: Only one of the 700 consumers interviewed commented about the outage. The market introduction went forward as planned. The test market was a success.

Case Study #2: Package Design Research

A manufacturer wanted to improve the image of its liquid product. To do this, they were about to change both the bottle and the label. They were not changing the product. Conventional, mall intercept, consumer tests were conducted. The results indicated that the changes should not be made. When, however, the new bottle/label product was taken and placed on store shelves and the exact same interview used in the mall study was conducted, the results of the in-store interviews were dramatically different from the mall test. The package changes were well received in-store, and management went forward with the changes. The introduction of the new bottle/label was considered a success.

Case Study #3: Capital-Intensive Product Form Change

A radical form change was being considered for a cleaning product, and a conventional simulated test market (STM) was conducted. The results were neither encouraging nor discouraging. There was, however, a major capital expense involved in moving forward with this initiative. With these results, management could not justify the expense involved with the change. An in-store test was conducted, with the results being dramatically favorable. The project went forward, with product change setting a new standard for the category. Five years later, all major category participants had modified their brands to duplicate the change.

Case Study #4: Package Design Research

A major detergent manufacturer was about to make a major change in the bottle and label of a cleaning product. Conventional test methods encouraged the change. However, one skeptic in the company was holding out on the change, which was a dramatic departure from their current bottle and label. An in-store "shelf appearance test" was requested, using the very same interview used in the conventional testing. The results of the in-store study proved disastrous for the new bottle and label combination. Even before the results were tabulated, however, the initiative was canceled. The marketing research director was present at the testing and heard both the reactions of the shoppers and saw the shelf appearance of the brand. In the conventional testing, the brand was displayed with light on all sides of the bottle, giving it a "halo" appearance. On the store shelf, however, there was no backlighting. The result was a very poor appearance. As one respondent put it, "It looked like dirty motor oil."

In consumer research, it pays to consider the possible physical and psychological biases involved in your test designs. My experience is that "Assessment in Context" leads to more successes and less financial risk.

Can you imagine trying to assess pricing structures of products sitting on a table in the back room of a mall? How typical is that of the natural environment? Maybe it is typical of research, but not of the consumer's natural environment of product prices. How about testing the appearance of a container sitting on a table and not on a store shelf? It's like testing a car's driving comfort while sitting in it on the showroom floor.

For years, Sorensen Associates has been using real stores to test consumer products. Actually, 90+% of their studies are conducted in the retail environment. That's why they are called the "In-Store Research Company." While at Procter & Gamble, I was heavily involved in using the consumer's home and the store environment as my laboratory. P&G was using homes before I ever came on board, and that was in 1951. I believe Dr. Smelser, the creator of the Market Research Department in 1923, used the consumer's home as the base of all his research. In the 1970s, we started using real stores as focal points for assessing brand images, brand choices, package design, pricing, purchase motivation, brand rejection, and so on.

It's called Assessment in Context. I think it is all about reliability and validity of the research.

Index

Note: Page numbers followed by *n* are located in the footnotes.

in-store research
  eye-tracking research, 50-53
  importance of, 3-4
  pioneering work in, 1-3
  shopping time
    average shopping time per week, 8-10
    shopper seconds per dollar, 10-11
  tracking shoppers' eye movements and field of vision, 5-8
  value of, 20-22
incremental purchase, Marsh Supermarkets case study, 186-187
inefficiency, power of, 87
information acceleration, 150
Information Resources, Inc. (IRI) VideoCart, 192-193
instinctive-distinctive paths, 39-41
Institute of Marketing Science, 31
interacting with shoppers, 191
  implications of new technology, 194-195
  shopper loyalty cards, 21
  via cell phones, 193-194
  via VideoCart, 192-193
Internet influence on shopping behavior, 148-149
intrinsic value, 117
IRI (Information Resources, Inc.) VideoCart, 192-193

J-K

Jewel-Osco, movement to downsize stores, 25
Juran, Joseph, 112*n*

King Kullen, 99
knowledge-building visits, 156
Korzenny, Betty Ann, 169
Korzenny, Felipe, 169
Kvickly supermarket, 119

L

La Curacao case study, 174-175
Latino shoppers. *See* **Hispanic shoppers**
layered merchandising, 38-39
layout of stores, 85-88
leader products, 107
left-entry stores, 76
Leonard, Stew, 11-13, 61, 93, 194
licensing, 152
Lidl, growth of, 25-26
limited selection strategy, 12
location hypothesis, 80
long tail, 33
loyalty cards, 21, 169

M

Machado, Antonio, 69
Magellan, 192
main (primary) store, 88-90